WHEN

YOUR

SOUL

ACHES

LOIS MOWDAY RABEY

WHEN YOUR SOUL ACHES

HOPE AND HELP *for* WOMEN
WHO HAVE LOST THEIR HUSBANDS

WATERBROOK
PRESS

WHEN YOUR SOUL ACHES
PUBLISHED BY WATERBROOK PRESS
12265 Oracle Boulevard, Suite 200
Colorado Springs, Colorado 80921

All scripture quotations, unless otherwise indicated, are taken from the *Holy Bible, New International Version*®. NIV®. Copyright © 1973, 1978, 1984 by International Bible Society. Used by permission of Zondervan Publishing House. All rights reserved.

ISBN 978-0-307-73022-0

Published in association with the literary agency of Alive Communications, Inc., 7680 Goddard Street, Suite 200, Colorado Springs, Colorado 80920.

Published in the United States by WaterBrook Multnomah, an imprint of the Crown Publishing Group, a division of Random House Inc., New York.

WATERBROOK and its deer colophon are registered trademarks of Random House Inc.

Library of Congress Cataloging-in-Publication Data
Rabey, Lois Mowday.
    When your soul aches : hope and help for women who have lost their husbands / by Lois Mowday Rabey.—1st ed.
        p. cm.
    ISBN-13: 978-0-307-73022-0
    1. Widows—Life skills guides. 2. Widows—Religious life. I. Title.

HQ1058 .R33 2000

305.48'9654—dc21   00-035941

Printed in the United States of America

2000—First Edition

10 9 8 7 6 5 4 3 2 1

For all women who have suffered the loss of a spouse,

with special love to

ELSIE MILLER

Contents

PART I: IN THE EARLY DAYS OF LOSS

Section Six: "How Do I Deal with Other People?"

PART II: WHEN YOU'RE READY
TO MOVE AHEAD

Section Seven: "How Do I Move on with My Life?"

Section Eight: "What About Men?"

Section Nine: "What Does the Future Hold?"

Acknowledgments

I've had the privilege of working with the same people on several book projects. Familiarity doesn't lessen my gratitude for the assistance and care I continue to receive from these competent writing and publishing professionals: Kathy Yanni, Liz Heaney, and all the people at WaterBrook Press.

To the Tuesday morning ladies group—you are the greatest! Thank you for your prayers and cheerleading: Carol Donaldson, Cathy Eskew, Lynn Ganz, Judi Shive, Susan Wyatt, and Jan Zimmerman.

To my family, all of whom continually encourage and support me—you are bright lights in my life and bring me joy beyond what you could possibly know. Thank you!

And a special thank-you to all the widows I have met with over the years. You know who you are, and you remember, along with me, the times we sat and talked and cried together. Your openness and courage have been an ongoing encouragement to me. I pray that you are continually blessed with God's hope and love.

My Story, Your Story

I have been where you are: widowed, sad, angry, shocked, frightened, comforted, hopeful, lost…confused. I know how alone you can feel.

My first husband, Jack, died more than twenty years ago, but I remember well the day of his death. That event has affected my life ever since.

It was December 15, 1979. Our daughters, Lisa and Lara, and I had purchased a ride in a hot-air balloon as a Christmas present for Jack. We were all excited, and the girls had even managed to keep quiet about the big secret!

The south Florida morning was clear and crisp, a perfect morning for the balloon launch. I had invited two of Jack's close friends and business associates, Glenn Berg and Rick Rhine, to join him on this adventure. After gathering at our house early in the morning and rousting Jack from sleep, Glenn and Rick piled into our station wagon along with our family, Glenn's wife, Gail, and Rick's fiancée, Kathy, and we headed to suburban Fort Lauderdale.

In short order we were at the launch site and the balloon was ready for takeoff. The girls and I waved excitedly from below as the three men and the pilot ascended. We snapped pictures and hurriedly climbed back into the car to follow the balloon. The girls and I were exhilarated. Then it happened. Sheer joy disintegrated into sheer horror in a matter of seconds when the balloon hit power lines and a flame shot out from the side of the basket. I pushed Lisa and Lara down to the floor of the front seat of the car to shield them from the horrifying scene. I watched in disbelief as two men jumped from the burning basket. The balloon rose dramatically as the flames heated the air. Two more people fell before the roaring fire consumed the remains of the wicker basket.

I raced from the car and knelt first beside Glenn's body, not knowing where Jack's had landed. For a few mysterious and unexplainable moments, I felt only peace and the comfort of God's presence. I had no fear or dread or even pain. In that moment God miraculously wrapped me in his arms and showered me with a glimpse of heaven.

God was present in a real and comforting way at this terrible moment, and I knew he would continue to be with us. His tender ministrations would carry me through the early trials of widowhood. They did not erase the pain and struggle, but they gave me hope. No matter what the future held for my children and me, I believed we would not be alone.

My loss was shockingly sudden. Jack and I were both thirty-four years old and in excellent health when he was killed. We had anticipated many long years together.

Was your loss also sudden? Was your husband the victim of an accident, a sudden heart attack, an unexpected stroke? Or did he suffer through the long agony of a terminal illness?

Regardless of the circumstances surrounding your husband's death, the result is the same. Your husband has died. You are a widow. I was a widow. Each of our situations is personal—unique—and yet we share the experience of loss. I want you to know that you are not alone on this journey.

My heart longs to comfort and encourage you, to validate your feelings, and to bring you hope for the days ahead. I have sat at many a kitchen table with other widows as we've cried and laughed together. We have spoken in hushed tones about feelings only we can understand. We have prayed. We have sat in silence. We have shared a sweet communion with each other.

I've tried to capture the essence of those conversations within the pages of this book. I have included other insights as well, insights that might have helped me had I known them when I first became a widow. Part 1 addresses the immediate feelings and needs we face in the early days of loss. Every widow I talk with wants to know: "Why did this happen? Will I always feel this way? Are there things I should be doing? Am I going to get through this?" Part 2 looks ahead to the time when you will be ready to move on and to forge a new future for yourself and your children.

All of the stories in this book are from my own life or from the experiences of widows who agreed to let me tell their stories. Some of the women were young when they lost their husbands, some older. Each entry stands alone, and they can be read in any order.

I pray that your heart will find healing as you wander through these pages.

PART I

IN THE EARLY
DAYS OF LOSS

"Will I Always Hurt This Deeply?"

One Step at a Time

Are you asking yourself *Will I make it through this?* Most widows do. Your life has been turned upside down, and the adjustments are daunting. For months after Jack's death, I carried around a seemingly endless to-do list on a yellow legal pad, but that list covered only what needed to be done to settle Jack's business affairs. It didn't address things that needed to be done concerning the kids, the house, the cars, or the finances.

The early days after loss can be overwhelming. You'll hear conflicting advice. You'll have difficulty making decisions about things that seem simple, let alone decisions that are complex or involve matters foreign to you. Some of the best advice I received in those tumultuous days was to slow down and wait on God to give me direction.

A missionary friend's story of a South American tribe illustrates this principle. For some reason, this group moved about only at night. Because they lived in a rugged area that was dotted with steep cliffs, their nighttime journeys were dangerous. But they solved their dilemma by carrying makeshift lanterns that cast just enough light to see one step ahead. As long as they walked slowly and kept their eyes on the lighted ground, they kept on the path. By walking only one step at a time, they were able to keep from falling off a precipice.

Some days you may feel like you are moving through a similarly threatening land. You'll feel lost and afraid of taking a misstep. But if you move slowly and keep your eyes on God, he will help you make wise choices. Take time to consider and evaluate the advice you are given. Spend time with God, asking his specific direction for each step you take. He promises to be with you and to guide you.

> *Show me your ways, O LORD,*
> *teach me your paths;*
> *guide me in your truth and teach me,*
> *for you are God my Savior,*
> *and my hope is in you all day long.*
>
> PSALM 25:4-5

"When Will Life Get Back to Normal?"

From the morning of Jack's accident until the evening of the memorial service, friends, neighbors, and out-of-town guests steadily flowed through my home. I had to make the funeral arrangements, plan the memorial service, and meet with the many people who supported and comforted the girls and me.

Five days after Jack died, the flurry of activity simply stopped. Only a few close friends remained. Most people had to get back to their jobs and families and things to do; they had to get back to life as normal. I had to go to Jack's office and meet with attorneys and insurance agents. Jack had operated his own insurance agency, and Glenn and Rick were the only agents who worked with him. The accident had wiped out the entire agency at once, leaving me with a huge mess to untangle.

As I drove over to the office that day, I thought, *I'll get this meeting out of the way, and then get back to normal.* But eight hours and sixteen yellow legal-pad pages later, I realized "normal" wouldn't be happening for a long time.

Are you, too, wondering when life will seem normal again?

In the early days of loss, there is little in your life that qualifies as normal. Everything revolves around your loss. You have to attend to legal matters regarding your husband's business affairs and establish yourself as the responsible party for your family. Every day you will be faced with new decisions about your children, your home, your finances, your car, and more. Many of these practical matters are addressed in this book. Try to remember that the feeling of being drowned by changes will subside.

You will feel out-of-joint for a long time. That's okay. In time you will adjust. You will feel normal again, but *normal* won't look the same as before. It will be a new kind of normal.

> *Be strong and take heart, all you who hope in the* Lord.

Psalm 31:24

"What Did He Feel?"

I didn't see Jack's body after the accident, but the coroner's report detailed the cause of death. As I held the lengthy document in my hands, an attorney who was with me suggested that I might not want to read it.

"Tell me what you think his last moments were like," I asked the attorney. He told me that Jack's hands had been badly burned which probably meant that he held on until he passed out, never even being aware that he was falling.

For weeks I played a horrific scene over and over again in my mind. I would look at the burners on the stove and imagine holding my hands on the red-hot coils until I passed out. It was torture.

Then one day I asked a close family friend who is a doctor to explain to me what it might have been like for Jack in the midst of that much pain and panic. My friend gently and reassuringly told me that the body has mechanisms that override pain in life and death situations. In my simplistic understanding I think he meant that pain is not experienced by someone in that situation the same way it would be for someone just thinking about the situation. We cannot project what terminal pain would feel like because the physiological responses present for the person are not present for us.

Jack was undoubtedly trying to think of a way to survive and that thought allowed him to hold on even though his hands were holding on to a burning material.

I have another friend whose husband died a very painful death as a result of cancer. His last days were agony. She told me that, although she desperately wanted him to be healed, she was relieved when the pain was over for him. She didn't play those last weeks over in her mind but focused on the peace that death brought him.

I think the best way to release the torturing mental images of a loved one's last moments is to remember that they were not only experiencing physical responses that we can't imagine, but that they were also the recipients of supernatural grace that carried them from this world to the next.

SCENT OF A MEMORY

Long before aromatherapy was popular, I loved fragrances. I've worn perfume since I was a young girl, and I've loved the smell of aftershave and men's cologne since sniffing my father's familiar bottle of Old Spice.

Jack wore an aftershave called Royal Copenhagen. Its crystal-blue liquid came in a clear bottle with a blue-and-silver cap. He would pour a small amount into his cupped hand, clap his hands together, and then lightly slap both sides of his face as droplets splashed onto the bathroom countertop. Sometimes he'd quietly come up behind me; I'd get a whiff of Royal Copenhagen and know he was there. The handle on his leather briefcase held traces of that fragrance. When I ironed his shirts, the steam from his collars brought his scent into my presence even though he wasn't there.

After Jack's death I savored those moments when I would capture his scent from his clothes or briefcase. And after I took his clothes out of the closet and put his briefcase in storage, I'd sometimes sprinkle drops of Royal Copenhagen from his half-used bottle onto my pillowcase. I'd bury my head in the pillow and inhale deeply. And then I'd cry for a long time.

In the days ahead, many things will remind you of your husband. Don't be afraid to embrace them. You need to remember him and your life together. Good memories can be healing.

"After Forty-Five Years, He's Gone"

Elsie lost her husband of forty-five years after a brief bout with cancer. Her five grown sons and their families are spread across the country from the East Coast to the West Coast, and she is in the midland of Missouri. She is grateful for frequent contact with her children and grandchildren, but she talked to me of the strangeness that accompanies the loss of a lifetime mate. "I really miss having someone to care if I had a good day or to tell news to or to talk things over with. It's hard, too, coping with a couples' world and not fitting in with anybody."

As she told me how difficult the weekends are, particularly Sundays, I remembered all too well that isolated feeling when sitting in a church pew surrounded by other families. Elsie had spent nearly a half-century sitting next to the same man in church and listening to him sing a solo or preach a sermon. She told me, "It's difficult, but my hope is that I can minister to other women who have lost a husband. I want to be a good witness to the fact that God is in control of my situation."

The loss of a spouse after so many years not only leaves a huge emotional void, but also prompts changes in a long-established lifestyle. Over the years two people become so connected that the death of one leaves the other adrift. Elsie, like other women who have lost a spouse later in life, is moving on. She still hurts, but she is coping and growing.

If you have lost a life partner, hang on to hope. Like Elsie, you will survive. Your pain will lessen. You will experience joy again.

"When will the pain go away?" Julie asked me. Her husband had died suddenly, leaving her with an infant and a toddler to rear alone.

"I'm afraid all of the pain doesn't go away," I answered softly. "But it does lessen, and peace increases."

Julie thought that God's peace meant the absence of pain. She believed that if she could just do enough of the right spiritual things, she would find comfort and no longer feel the pain of loss.

Scripture never promises Christians a pain-free life. Instead, the Bible is filled with words and phrases like *perseverance, endurance, finishing the race,* and *standing firm to the end,* and we miss their implication. Life involves pain—that's why we need perseverance, endurance, and encouragement to keep on keeping on. But in the midst of our deepest pain, God's inexpressible peace invades our hearts and brings us joy in the sorrow.

As the years pass, you will experience more joy and less pain, but the loose threads of grief will come up every now and then, reminding you of your loss. Fourteen years after Jack died, my daughter Lara married. She and Craig were married in southern California on a beautiful, sunny day in mid-December. The bridal party arrived at the church several hours before the ceremony to take pictures. Lara and her bridesmaids had dressed in one of the parlor rooms of the church amid a flurry of girl-talk and makeup. They had moved outside for photos in the courtyard, and I had stayed behind to make sure nothing essential was left behind.

As I came out of the dressing room, I saw Lara posed for the camera. Suddenly she flinched and broke her pose; tears spilled down her face. Just then, I saw her Uncle Bud, who bears a striking resemblance to Jack, walk up and hug her. Neither of them said a word. They smiled and cried, looking at each other knowingly.

That poignant moment held both peace and pain. In that moment a daughter and a brother shared the pain of loss and the absolute joy of Lara's wedding. The pain didn't ruin the day, nor did it diminish the peace. And the very touch of God transformed the pain into peace.

No, pain doesn't completely go away this side of heaven, so there's no point in trying to run from it. Accept it and ask God to touch those deeply painful places of your soul with his love.

> *Because of the tender mercy of our God,*
> *by which the rising sun will come to us from*
> *heaven*
> *to shine on those living in darkness*
> *and in the shadow of death,*
> *to guide our feet into the path of peace.*
>
> Luke 1:78-79

"MY HUSBAND MADE ALL THE DECISIONS"

"I was a 1950s kind of wife," Betty told me. "Even though John and I did everything together, he made all the final decisions. I don't say this in a detrimental way. I loved the thirty-eight years when I didn't have to make the decisions."

The loss of her lifelong companion forced Betty into a steep learning curve. "I'm learning accounting, how to buy and sell a car, how to invest in mutual funds, how to hire and manage people to work on my house and car. I didn't do any of these things before. I have to decide how much money is enough to live on, do I stay in the house or move, and if I move, where?"

Betty's first six months of widowhood were horrible, and she found herself in a deep pit of hopelessness. "It was terrible to see the empty chair where John would have sat, to eat alone. An intense loneliness and despair almost swallowed me. Then I made a decision that changed my despair to hope. I decided to let God walk me through this, and I began to move one step at a time. I chose to not be bitter." Today Betty facilitates grief workshops and is involved in ministry at her church. Her pain no longer consumes her.

It's doubly overwhelming to lose a husband and simultaneously to be faced with decisions you have never wrestled with on your own. Make an intentional decision to believe that you will live through this. Allow God to come next to you and show you the way. Ask him to fill you with hope and a desire to live well as a woman full of life.

> *You are my hiding place;*
> *you will protect me from trouble*
> *and surround me with songs of deliverance.*
>
> PSALM 32:7

No "Right" Way to Grieve

Americans subscribe to an unwritten rule that says mourning should last a year, and then our hearts should be healed. I was told that once I had gone through our anniversary, Jack's birthday, and all the major holidays, I would feel much better. Not true! Some days *were* better, but others were painful...for a long time.

Grief resists all labels. It isn't linear. We don't progress neatly from one stage of grief to the next. Grief is messy, bewildering, and encompasses a range of emotions. I would feel easily excited one moment and down in the dumps the next. Just when I felt I had overcome some fear, it would sneak back into my thinking.

Your journey through grief is unique. Many of the thoughts you read in this book will express exactly how you feel. Others will seem foreign. That's okay. There isn't a "right" way to grieve. It is a process, but it is an individual process. So in the days ahead, feel what you feel and don't be concerned if your experience differs from that of others.

Denial Is Normal

Many years ago, one of Jack's friends from helicopter flight school was killed in Vietnam. His body was never recovered, and only his dog tags were returned to his widow. Jack was a pallbearer at the funeral. At the graveside the widow threw herself on the coffin and begged for someone to open it so she could see her husband, but there was no body to show her. Her tears and pleadings filled the air with her pain. She wanted some evidence of her husband's death so that she could really believe it. How I ached for her!

Many women experience denial, even those who are present at the time of death. Denial gives you time to adjust to the wrenching loss of your spouse. Intellectually you know your husband has died, but emotionally that reality is too horrifying to embrace right away. That's okay. You may have moments when you expect your husband to walk in the door any minute. Or you may dream that your husband is still alive or that he didn't *really* die in the accident or in the hospital.

But denial can be unhealthy if it becomes a way of life. If you act as if your husband is still alive—talking to him, pretending he is with you, living in a fantasy—you may need professional help. Check with your pastor for a referral to a Christian counselor or with friends who may know someone to recommend. Also check with churches in your area to see if any offer grief workshops you could attend.

Denial is normal. It comes and goes, and in time it disappears completely.

"Where Is My Husband When I Need Him?"

Math frustrates me, so Jack always balanced our books. When he was gone, I had to learn to balance them myself. I put if off as long as I could.

Finally, I sat at the dining room table with bills and papers spread in front of me. Lisa and Lara were tucked into bed, and I had planned to balance the checkbook for the first time in my life. I gave myself what I thought was a reasonable amount of time to follow the steps listed on the back of my latest statement. It wasn't long before I was fuming. My figures just didn't match the bank's balance. I worked through the steps again. Still a significant discrepancy.

"Where are you, Jack! I need you!" I said loudly. I was angry—angry that he left me, angry that I had to do something I hated and couldn't do well, angry that my days of having a partner to share the load were over. I was angry with Jack for dying and leaving me alone.

I knew my ire was futile, and it didn't last long. But I felt it, expressed it out loud, laughed at myself, and then attacked the checkbook again. I never did reconcile the figures that evening. The next day I went to the bank and found a sympathetic person who balanced the account for me and showed me how to do it.

Every widow I've met has been angry at her husband for dying and leaving her alone, even though her husband didn't choose to die, didn't desert her in the usual sense of the word, didn't actually do anything to incur her wrath. But she is angry with him anyway.

Many of us are also angry with God. We are angry that God allowed this tragedy to happen. We are mad because he didn't intervene. He could have, so why didn't he? Such questions, asked sincerely, can lead to healing. God receives our anger and returns love. We often feel better after we've vented.

If you feel anger bubbling out of your frustration and pain, let it out. Don't let it build. Get it out and clear the way for God's touch of love to come in and calm you.

> *The* LORD *longs to be gracious to you;*
> *he rises to show you compassion.*
> *For the* LORD *is a God of justice.*
> *Blessed are all who wait for him!*

ISAIAH 30:18

If Only...

The girls and I gave Jack, Glenn, and Rick the balloon ride as a present. They died as a result of our gift. I can't count the number of times I thought, *If only we hadn't bought that balloon ride...*

The words *if only* often haunt those of us who are left behind. These words produce guilt and generate deep feelings of remorse and regret. Even if we don't feel guilt about circumstances surrounding the death, we usually feel guilt over unsaid words or words said in anger. We wish we'd done something differently.

We seem to think that if we could live our marriage over, we would live it perfectly. In reality, we all make mistakes, say things that hurt others, and miss opportunities to be loving and affirming.

But, you may be thinking, *I did some spiteful things that I would take back if I only had the chance. I do regret my attitude toward my husband a lot of the time.* If this is the case, you may need to ask God's forgiveness and then forgive yourself.

Though you can't turn back the clock, you can improve the relationships you are in today. You can learn from mistakes and grow as a result. Let yourself grieve the things you wish you had done differently, learn from them, and forgive yourself.

What's Your Way of Coping?

I responded to the unexpected—and unwanted—responsibilities that used to be Jack's by charging ahead. I felt more in control when I was busy, so I plowed on. My activity carried its own set of challenges: I sometimes made decisions too quickly; I often ran on adrenaline and then crashed; and I neglected my need to take time to grieve and take care of myself. My life was out of balance, but I wasn't about to let grief get me down!

Fortunately, I had people around me who cautioned me to slow down. They advised me not to make major decisions—like selling the house or moving—for at least a year. They reminded me that I needed to spend both quantity and quality time with my children. They encouraged me to pace myself and to give my body, mind, and spirit time to heal and be restored.

Some women who are overwhelmed with grief respond in the opposite way. Instead of filling their lives with action, they stay in bed. The painful emotions of widowhood eventually overpower them, and they become chronically depressed.

If determination to survive keeps you busy, busy, busy, running on adrenaline—take a breath. Stop and evaluate your pace. Talk with some friends about how to moderate your activity so it's healthy, allowing time for your family, your health, and your spiritual nourishment.

If you can't get out of bed, handle even the smallest of life's chores, or think clearly, enlist the help of your friends. Ask them to help you find a counselor or grief recovery group. Invite your friends to walk through this journey with you. If you don't have anyone in your life who can walk alongside you and lend support, then call some churches and ask about support groups for widows. This may sound risky, but you will heal much more quickly with the help of others.

One Day, You'll Feel Ready to Move On

On November 4, 1979, fifty-two Americans were taken hostage when Iranian militants stormed the U.S. Embassy in Teheran. Newspapers and television offered daily accounts of their continuing ordeal. People tied yellow ribbons around trees, mailboxes, and light posts—any object they could—across the front yards of America. Jack and I followed the story and prayed for the safe return of the hostages. Every day we listened to the radio and television reports and scanned the newspapers for updates.

One day in May after Jack's death, I opened the newspaper and was surprised to see a story about the hostages. I had not read one newspaper or tuned in to a single television show since Jack's death on December 15, and I had forgotten all about the hostages. Grief and responsibility had consumed me. I had nothing left for anyone or anything outside my immediate family. Our loss had absorbed all my thoughts and feelings. Even the biggest news story of the day had escaped my notice.

I didn't feel guilty, but I did sense a desire to reconnect, to emerge from my cocoon.

In the months ahead, you will be absorbed with your loss. Don't feel badly about this. Your feelings are normal. There is no prescribed timetable for grief. Eventually you will want to reconnect with others; in time your ache will lessen and you will begin to heal.

Weeping may remain for a night, but rejoicing comes in the morning.

PSALM 30:5

26

"Are There Things I Should Be Doing?"

PRAY

When I first became a widow, prayer took on a fresh meaning. Instead of setting aside a specific time to pray, I prayed throughout the day, constantly conversing with God about what I was feeling or experiencing. Stripped of any illusion of self-sufficiency, I was deeply aware that I needed God's help with everything from breathing to buying cars. Prayer became not only a holy endeavor, but also a necessary ingredient in learning to live with God as my husband.

How else could I survive, let alone make wise decisions?

Ironically, when people ask what they can do to help, many widows reply, "All you can do is pray," as if prayer is of lesser value than cooking meals or driving carpools. Sometimes this answer comes from a heart that is aware of our absolute dependence on God for everything, and other times it comes from a sense of exasperation that we are not in control of our lives. It's as if prayer is the ugly stepsister on our list of significant helps. Yet prayer is the most practical thing you can do to guide you through this maze of widowhood.

If you realize, for example, that some important bill has inadvertently gone unpaid, don't panic, pray. Prayer can't write the check and satisfy the creditor, but prayer can give you the presence of mind to deal with the situation.

If you can't find the title to your husband's pickup and can't transfer the truck to your name without it, don't panic, pray. Prayer won't make the title pop out of its hiding place in the files, but prayer can give you the calmness to assess the situation and let options occur to you. Perhaps you'll be inspired to call the Department of Motor Vehicles for assistance. Or perhaps a friend can tell you how to obtain an official copy.

Be assured that God hears your prayers. When you seek him, God offers great comfort and wisdom.

> *"For I know the plans I have for you," declares the LORD, "plans to prosper you and not to harm you, plans to give you hope and a future. Then you will call upon me and come and pray to me, and I will*

listen to you. You will seek me and find me when
you seek me with all your heart."

JEREMIAH 29:11-13

❧

GO AHEAD AND CREATE A MEMORIAL

I love pictures and have always taken photographs. Numerous albums and boxes of photos document every major event of my life, and many minor ones. Shortly after Jack died, I selected dozens of my favorite pictures of him and had them enlarged: pictures from his high-school and college basketball days, pictures of him in his army reserve uniform, pictures of us together, pictures of him with the girls. These photographs chronicled our life together.

I displayed all of them. Every wall and table in our house had visual reminders of Jack. Anyone who entered the house knew that the man captured so frequently on film was revered, loved, and missed. In those early days, these pictures comforted me. I wanted to see him at every turn. I wanted to remember.

Don't be afraid to remember. Surround yourself with things

that remind you of your husband and of your life together. You can put them away later. For now, display as many as you want.

GETTING RID OF THE BED

About a year before Jack died, we purchased a king-size waterbed. I hadn't wanted one, but Jack was persistent, so I finally relented. Even he agreed it wasn't as blissful as he'd expected. For one thing, our weight difference created a problem for us. We couldn't get the water level adjusted properly. If the water level was too low, we'd roll toward the middle. If it was too high, we'd both rest on top of a slightly rounded surface. We finally settled on a level that allowed both of us to be fairly comfortable. Jack delighted in our seaworthy cradle, but I did not!

The night of his accident, I couldn't bring myself to sleep alone in our bed. No longer would I roll into him in the middle of the bed or sleep perched on top of the firmer side of the mattress. That first night I slept on the sofa bed in our family room.

It's funny how silly arguments can become the source of great longing. I would have gladly claimed my side of our waterbed if it meant sharing it with Jack again.

Many of the challenges of widowhood have to be met: Children need to be raised, finances handled, cars repaired, yard work tackled. But some challenges can be tossed rather than confronted day after day. I tossed the bed. It reminded me of playful sparring over a mild disagreement that I would have loved to tangle over again.

Is there some possession you need to toss? Don't be hasty, but don't feel you have to keep everything either.

Write Down Comforting Scripture Verses

Despite today's technological sophistication, I still use pen or pencil to record my thoughts and experiences. My day-planner has a section of blank pages, which I write in frequently. It's not an electronic-miracle data-keeper, and I like it that way. There is something therapeutic about thoughts moving from my mind, through my fingers, and onto a page.

At the time I became a widow, technology as we know it now was a dream of the future. So if a verse comforted and strengthened me, I wrote it in longhand on an index card and carried it with me. My stack of cards grew so large that I put them in a little metal index box and carried it with me.

I suggest you consider doing the same: Copy by hand the words of God that fill you with hope, joy, and peace and remind you of his love. Write down the words that settle your painful emotions and fill your heart with the evidence that God fulfills his promises.

Many of the verses I recorded professed God's presence with me even when I felt he was far away. As long as I could believe he was really near—despite my feelings—I felt like I would make it through those difficult days. These are a few that comforted me:

As I was with Moses, so I will be with you; I will never leave you nor forsake you. (Joshua 1:5)

Keep me as the apple of your eye; hide me in the shadow of your wings. (Psalm 17:8)

I am still confident of this: I will see the goodness of the LORD in the land of the living. Wait for the LORD; be strong and take heart and wait for the LORD. (Psalm 27:13-14)

Weeping may remain for a night, but rejoicing comes
in the morning. (Psalm 30:5)

As it is written: "No eye has seen, no ear has heard, no
mind has conceived what God has prepared for those
who love him." (1 Corinthians 2:9)

Which verses comfort you? Which ones bring you hope? Write
them down and keep them with you. (At the back of this book is
an additional list of comforting scriptures.) They will help you
claim the truth even when your emotions draw you away from it.
Believing what God says makes a difference.

RECORD YOUR FEELINGS

I'd encourage you to make use of a journal as a cathartic tool.
Writing down your feelings will help you weave through the tangle
of emotions. You will understand yourself better as you put words
to your emotions and find relief as you articulate them.

In the intensity of the moment, all of us think we will never forget how we feel or how God is moving on our behalf. But our memories dim as time passes. Journal entries provide a written record of our progress and God's intervention. We can read about yesterday's struggles and compare them with where we are today.

In the early days of widowhood, for example, I wrote down my fears about rearing my children alone. After some weeks had passed, I became aware that I felt more confident as a single parent. I wrote that the girls were adjusting and that we were establishing a fulfilling home, just the three of us. As I looked back through my journal, I could recall the fear, read about the changes in our lives, and see how far I had come from fear to confidence. This written record affirmed my faith. God had heard my cries for help!

Plan a day to go to several stationery stores or bookstores and pick out a lovely blank book in which you can record your feelings. Write anything, everything. Just let it all out—plan, ponder, ramble. If you just hate to write, I can only encourage you to give it a try. Maybe you would prefer to record your feelings and thoughts on a computer. That's okay too.

Widowhood is a dense jungle in the early years. Writing can help you unravel some of the internal tangle by enabling you to think in new ways, see from different perspectives, and grow into the woman God wants you to be.

Give it a try.

Get Your Paperwork Organized ASAP

The morning after Jack's memorial service, I met with attorneys, insurance agents, our pastor, and a financial advisor in Jack's office, now eerily empty. The custodian had been coming in daily and putting all the mail on Jack's desk. It had grown to a precarious pile. The letters on the top had begun to slide off and fall to the floor. I came in and sat in Jack's chair, dwarfed by the paper mountain in front of me. One of the men handed me a yellow legal pad and a pen. "You will need these," he said kindly, "to make a list."

Eight hours and eighteen pages later, I left the office with my to-do list. I felt overwhelmed, but also encouraged by those men who would spend the next year helping me sort out the legalities of closing the agency.

As we were leaving one of them reminded me to go down to the Social Security office and file a claim. Then he added that I should also get copies of the death certificate to send to businesses to inform them that I was assuming responsibility for our accounts: credit cards, the mortgage, the car payment.

I wasn't very organized in those days. I carried my yellow legal pad around and checked things off, but I didn't have a system for filing important papers. I tended to throw everything in a desk drawer, telling myself that someday soon the busywork would end.

But it doesn't.

I encourage you to get organized as soon as possible. If you have problems knowing how to do this, ask for help.

I wish I had. Begin with your friends who are experts in the areas where you are weak. Ask an accountant or bookkeeper to meet with you and help you set up a record-keeping system. If you have a personal computer but are not familiar with using it for record keeping, make a similar arrangement with an experienced computer user. Be respectful of other people's time and offer to pay them. Many people are more than willing to help if they just know you need it.

Become an Advocate for Yourself

I called the telephone company to ask them to take Jack's name off the bill and put my name on it. Naively, I didn't expect any problems.

"Mrs. Mowday, you will need to send us four hundred dollars to continue your phone service," a woman on the other end of the phone told me matter-of-factly.

"What?" I replied, thinking that I misunderstood her.

"You will have to send us four hundred dollars to continue your phone service."

"Why?" I asked in disbelief.

She explained that I was opening a new account, and because our old telephone bills had run more than several hundred dollars a month, I would have to give the equivalent of a two-month deposit. We had never been late with any payment, and I didn't see how changing the name on our account constituted opening a new account. But she was unmoved. I asked if she could just add the deposit to my next bill, and she said no, and that I would need to send a check in or bring one to the local office in person. I had ten days to do so.

Though shocked and furious, I assumed I had no option but to comply.

A few days later, I received a phone call from the president of the local branch of the telephone company. He apologized profusely and said that no additional deposit would be required. When I asked him what had precipitated the change, he told me that my attorney had called him.

I must have relayed the story to my attorney in the course of a conversation, and he took the initiative to call the phone company on my behalf. My attorney also happened to be a Florida state representative.

"Thank you," I said. "But what happens to the people who don't have a state representative helping them?" There was silence on the other end of the phone. I realized I was being ungracious and apologized.

Businesses, for the most part, may be indifferent to your situation. If you encounter problems when changing the name on any of your bills or accounts, be respectful but firm about what you need. Seek help if you run into demands that seem unusual or that you are unable to meet. You will need to be your own advocate. This does not mean you have to become strident or aggressive, but you will need to be aware and wise.

Be as shrewd as snakes and as innocent as doves.

Matthew 10:16

Be Wise and Cautious
About Financial Affairs

Before Jack died, I was horribly ignorant about money matters. And I spent too much.

Many widows are provided for financially in their husband's will, giving them excess funds for the first time in their lives. Such a surplus can tempt you to spend more than is prudent, and it makes you vulnerable to the ploys of a money manager or investor who may not be acting in your best interest.

While there are many honest and well-meaning people in financial fields, some will put their own interests above yours. Because some of these people garner names from obituaries, it might be helpful to get an unlisted phone number to avoid a flood of unsolicited calls. Make sure that everyone with whom you do business provides references, and then check them. Friends can be helpful, but friendship can muddy the water of decision making. You may disagree about an investment but feel hesitant to express any reservation because of the friendship.

Managing finances requires discernment and assistance. Whatever your situation, I advise you to be cautious. Take your time before you make any financial decisions. Talk with those close to you who are knowledgeable. Read. Attend seminars, but be aware that many are sponsored by people who hope to sign you on as a client.

A wonderful resource for widows with excess funds is the ministry Royal Treasure. This organization was founded by a good friend of mine, Lu Dunbar, who worked in development with a number of Christian organizations for years. She met regularly with widows who were interested in giving to worthy causes. During the course of many conversations, Lu found that many widows had been taken advantage of financially. They had been ill advised by financial people and sought after by many solicitors looking for donations or investments—secular and Christian.

Royal Treasure offers information and seminars that help educate women on financial matters, with a specific emphasis on women who are making these decisions alone. The organization is located in Atlanta, Georgia. Lu may be contacted by e-mail at LuDunbar@royaltreasure.org or through her Web site: www.RoyalTreasure.org.

EARN A LIVING

But what if you were not left with adequate resources? If you are in this situation, your challenges are even more pressing. You may need to simplify your lifestyle or enter the workplace, perhaps for the first time or after an absence of many years.

Elaine, a widow in her early forties with three children, found herself in this situation when her husband died suddenly of a heart attack. His small insurance policy barely covered their living expenses for the first year. "Friends and the people at my church really helped out," she said. "They filled the gap until I could get a job, and then they continued to help with baby-sitting."

If you don't have friends or family nearby who can help you through this transition time, consider checking out some local churches where you might be able to get plugged in and receive spiritual, practical, and financial help. Also look in your local newspaper for churches that offer grief workshops and sign up for one. Usually those groups are well informed about available aid.

But don't rely on others as a long-term solution to your financial challenges. Talk with people about finding a job or getting the training or education you need to become marketable. In most larger cities, there are numerous classes for working adults that offer undergraduate and graduate degree programs that adapt to busy schedules. You will also find a variety of vocationally specific training courses that may suit your needs. Many of these are offered at a reasonable cost; check with your state department of education.

No matter how overwhelming this all sounds, you can navigate the challenges one step at a time. Begin where you are. Start talking, inquiring, listening, believing you can make a living, and moving toward this goal.

$$\sim\!\!\ll$$

EAT WELL

I couldn't eat anything solid for days after Jack died. A smorgasbord of food flowed into our home, but I couldn't get anything down. My only "nourishment" was coffee. Then one day something actually smelled inviting. One of my friends was heating a clear broth on the stove and told me that Nancy had delivered the soup earlier that day. The mild fragrance enticed me to accept a bowl, and I slowly sipped the warm liquid.

Someone commented that of all the wonderful, fancy foods that had come into the house, I had chosen the simplest. "Yes," I said, "and look who knew what to bring."

Nancy had lost a child some years before. She knew what it was like to almost gag when thinking about forcing solid food down your constricted throat. I felt a kinship with her and smiled at her sweet gift of a simple broth that nourished my soul as well as my body.

Your normal pattern of eating has undoubtedly been disrupted. You may be inclined to be obsessive either by eating too little or too much. Try to eat just a few sensible foods as you get through the early days. After a while you will again have the desire to eat well.

GET A PHYSICAL

About six months into my widowhood, some friends and I were talking one day about a stress test that had appeared in a women's magazine. One of the ladies had a copy of the test and gave it to me. I took it home and filled it out that night.

The test assigned points to different life events, and these points were an indicator of the amount of stress each event could produce. The article said that if you scored over three hundred points, you were considered in serious peril for stress-related maladies. I scored seven hundred points. Within a year, in addition to facing Jack's death, my father was diagnosed with cancer, my parents moved, and our dog died—and those were just the major stressors!

At the urging of my friends, I scheduled a routine physical. The doctor was kind and understanding, and he confirmed that it is a good idea to have a physical examination when you have been under so much emotional stress. All turned out to be well, and he even gave me a dispensation with regard to drinking coffee. He told me he felt it would be more stressful to ask me to quit than to allow me to continue one of my most pleasurable indulgences.

Even if you have no symptoms of illness, get a physical sometime within the first year of widowhood. If you have some specific concerns, such as insomnia, nervousness, anxiety, or weight gain or loss, be sure to mention them to your doctor.

FIND A HANDYMAN

We were remodeling our home when Jack died. He had been doing much of the work himself, so I was at a loss as to how to finish what he had started. Baseboards were off, walls were unpainted, and electrical work was incomplete.

I called several people listed in the phone book, but most declined to take on small, wrap-up jobs that someone else had started. One day some friends from church were visiting, and the husband looked around in dismay. When he realized that I had a number of unfinished jobs to be done around the house, he offered to help. He said that if I could be patient, he would try to work in the things I needed around his other jobs. I was so grateful that I leaped at his offer.

When the girls and I moved to Colorado, I found myself in the same predicament. We built a house, but when it was finished, I was unable to stay ahead of the repairs. This time another single woman referred me to a handyman. I hired him to hang outside Christmas lights, haul trash to the dump, and haul and stack wood. He did all sorts of odd jobs for me and proved invaluable.

Maybe you are very handy yourself and don't need such a person, but if not, put the word out with friends and at church. Visit your local hardware store and let them know you are looking for someone to help with odd jobs. Lots of people make a good living doing this and will be a great help to you. When inquiring, don't broadcast that you are living alone. Simply state that you are looking for help.

Take Safety Precautions

Vicki had been widowed about six months when the first letter arrived. She didn't recognize the handwriting, and there was no return address. The scrawled words were difficult to read, but as she deciphered them, she began to feel threatened. An unknown voyeur was writing to let her know that she and her children were being watched.

A very frightened Vicki continued to receive mail from this person for the next few months. All attempts to discover the writer failed. She got an unlisted number, installed an alarm system, and was diligent about locking doors. Eventually the letters stopped, but Vicki's sense of vulnerability lingered.

Single women can be targets for unwanted advances or attention. Lock your doors even if you live in a community where unlocked doors are the norm. Teach your children commonsense rules of safety. Don't become an alarmist, but do become careful. Combine wisdom about the world with your trust in God's watchful care.

"Should I Be Feeling This Way?"

"Why Did This Happen?"

We had a joint memorial service for Jack and the two friends who died with him. Because we all belonged to a large church, and because of the extensive news coverage of the accident, some people had to sit in an overflow section. A number who came didn't know the Lord. We were told later that many of those people accepted Christ as a result of the testimonies of these three men.

Even in death, those three lives influenced others to come to Christ. God truly blessed and comforted all of us with this good news.

Yet my primary question remained unanswered: *Why?* I was happy that people accepted Christ that day, but I also knew that God could have brought them to salvation another way. He could have intervened in the chain of events that led to these three deaths and, at the same time, brought those same people at the memorial service to a knowledge of himself in some other way.

If God had given me a choice between Jack's life and the lives of those people, I wouldn't have hesitated to choose Jack.

Why didn't God intervene and allow him and his two friends to live longer?

I don't believe we could ever find a reason that would satisfy us. Any explanation would still raise the question, *Why not do it differently, God?*

I have never faced a greater test of my faith than this. Would I keep demanding an answer that made sense or would I accept that God is both loving and all-powerful? Would I trust that God loves me? That he cares about me and Jack and our girls?

We can't explain why Christians suffer and die. Oh, we might be able to explain it theologically. We can say that all pain is the result of sin—if not our own, then Adam's. But we don't think it's fair that we should suffer because of something Adam did. And even so, the doctrine of sin doesn't explain why sometimes God intervenes and other times he doesn't.

While your "whys" may never be answered, it is possible to accept the paradox of God's sovereign love and his allowance of pain. Ask for the grace to live with unanswered questions and to relax in the comfort of gratitude when that grace flows into your life.

Oh, the depth of the riches of the wisdom and knowledge of God! How unsearchable his judgments, and his paths beyond tracing out!

ROMANS 11:33

"I'M SO ANGRY!"

"Sometimes I am so angry," Marie said to me, "and I know I shouldn't feel this way."

"Why not?" I asked.

"It isn't godly," she replied.

Marie and I talked about the feelings that flood us when we are adjusting to the loss of a spouse. At times we feel peace and comfort, and at other times we feel anger, fear, and doubt. And then we feel guilty, especially if we believe that Christians are supposed to be free from any negative emotions.

But emotions aren't right or wrong, good or bad. They are natural, human responses to the events and circumstances of life. The death of a spouse is a traumatic event that produces mixed emotions, many of them negative. But we can find healing in the experience and expression of negative feelings.

Jesus modeled emotional honesty with himself and God regarding his crucifixion. Scripture tells us that the night of his arrest: "He withdrew about a stone's throw beyond them, knelt down and prayed, 'Father, if you are willing, take this cup from me; yet not my will, but yours be done'" (Luke 22:41-42). Like Jesus, we can express our grief or anger. At the same time, like Jesus, we can accept the will of God for us.

There were days when I felt I should be "over" Jack's death, days when I wanted to forget about my feelings and get on with my life. But by God's grace I was surrounded by friends who kept reminding me that healing comes when we accept and embrace what we feel. They encouraged me to invite God into my healing. And I urge you to do the same.

Be honest about your feelings, and put yourself in God's hands. Express how you feel, grieve, and weep. Ask for God's healing and continue to wrestle with a confluence of emotions.

GUILT ABOUT FEELING GOOD

I met with Connie a few months after her husband had died from a heart attack. She greeted me warmly as we slid into a booth at a local restaurant. Before we even ordered, Connie looked cautiously over her shoulder, then leaned across the table. "I have been so eager to talk to you," she whispered. "I don't think anyone else could understand what I want to talk to you about." Connie began to pour out her feelings with a mixture of joy and guilt. "I have a fair number of days when I feel—well, good!"

Connie was aware that people sometimes see a widow's lifted spirits and wonder, *Doesn't she miss her husband? Has she forgotten him so quickly? Is she glad he's gone? Is she seeing another man already?* Ironically, these same people were probably praying that Connie would be comforted!

There will be days when you feel good—thank God for them. They are evidence that God heals in miraculous ways. Good days offer tangible hope that you really will live through this difficult time.

When you begin to feel better, give God the credit and don't worry about what other people think.

Praise be to the God and Father of our Lord Jesus
Christ! In his great mercy he has given us new birth

51

*into a living hope through the resurrection of Jesus
Christ from the dead, and into an inheritance that
can never perish, spoil or fade—kept in heaven for
you, who through faith are shielded by God's power
until the coming of the salvation that is ready to be
revealed in the last time.*

1 PETER 1:3-5

TIME DOESN'T HEAL ALL WOUNDS

When people quote the maxim that time heals all wounds, they
mean that if we just wait long enough the pain will go away. But
that is not true. The pain lessens, but it never goes away completely.

Just this past week I again felt the pain of losing Jack as I sat
in the stands at a state basketball tournament. My older daughter, Lisa, is the assistant coach for the girls' varsity basketball team
at the same school where she played basketball a decade ago, and
I had come to cheer her team on.

It was exciting to be back in the super-charged setting of high-school basketball play-offs. As the band played and the cheerleaders yelled, I was transported back to my own high-school days when I cheered for another star basketball player—the star that I would one day marry.

And thirteen short years later, he was taken from me.

I still feel pain every now and then. The pain is not as deep as it once was and it doesn't last as long, but it's there, a reminder that the loose threads of grief wisp around us for many years after our loss.

I have known some widows who suffer greatly many years after their loss because they don't allow God to touch them, to heal them. Instead of easing the pain, the passing years only prove to make them increasingly bitter.

Don't let that happen to you.

Healing does not mean we will experience no further pain. But your Father can comfort you. Stay close to him—always. He is the Great Physician. He wants you to have abundant life no matter what your circumstances, and he can bring healing that results in that abundance.

I have come that they may have life, and have it to the full.

JOHN 10:10

53

"God, Where Are You?"

Loneliness. It's the most painful part of losing your husband. You miss him specifically, and you miss the intimate companionship of another human being. Even the most introverted of us longs for close connection: to know and be known, to be accepted, to be understood. In human relationships, a healthy, loving marriage is the most likely relationship for this kind of intimacy to grow. When that relationship is gone, an enormous vacuum is created.

While children, friends, and family can help fill that void, only God can fill the emptiness. Recently I spoke to a group of singles about loneliness. After my opening talk, a woman raised her hand. She had tried to spend time with God to help her with her loneliness, she said, but she didn't feel his presence. "What do you do when you call out to God and there is silence?" she asked.

I wish I had an easy answer. I don't. Sensing God's presence takes time and persistence and faith. We relate to God in a different way than we do to each other. We don't see him with our eyes or hear him with our ears or touch him with our hands. We relate to God on a spiritual level, but that doesn't mean that he isn't present with us. He tells us that nothing can separate us from him, from his presence: "And surely I am with you always, to the very end of the age" (Matthew 28:20).

I love this passage of Scripture: "And I pray that you, being rooted and established in love, may have power, together with all the saints, to grasp how wide and long and high and deep is the love of Christ, and to know this love that surpasses knowledge—that you may be filled to the measure of all the fullness of God" (Ephesians 3:17-19). I want to know more of this love!

Sometimes I think that the best we can do is to just keep reminding ourselves that God is present, standing next to me, next to you. We can remember these verses, call him by name, and wait. If there is silence, we reaffirm what we know to be true. Like children, we trust that he does not leave us alone and forsaken.

When my grandson Justin had just learned to walk, I was baby-sitting him one day at his house. He was standing by his toy chest, and I was sitting on the sofa, reading a magazine. After a while, I got up and went into the kitchen to get a drink. As I opened the refrigerator, I noticed that it had gotten quiet in the living room. Before I could call to him, Justin called to me.

"Nana!" he cried out in an anxious voice.

"I'm right here, honey," I quickly replied, "in the kitchen." I could hear his little feet pattering across the living-room carpet as he ran to me. He threw his arms around my knees and held on tight.

Just because you can't see God doesn't mean he isn't present. God is with you all the time. You may not be aware of him or you may feel that he is far off, but he is near. When you are troubled, stop and, like a child, call out the name of Jesus. Wait long enough for his spirit to touch yours with the assurance of his presence. Believe he is with you even if you can't feel his nearness.

"HOW CAN I EVER TRUST AGAIN?"

One day shortly after Jack died, I was walking out of the house to pick up the girls at school. The phone rang, and I ran back in to answer it. The call was brief, but I was still a few minutes late to pick up Lisa and Lara. When I arrived they were waiting for me with anxious tears in their eyes.

"Where have you been, Mom?" they cried.

"I just took a phone call. I'm not that late."

While I tried to minimize their fear, I understood it. Even today, twenty years after Jack's accident, I'm fearful when my children are late in meeting me and when they are traveling on a plane or driving in a storm.

When someone you love dies unexpectedly or tragically, you can no longer say, "That will never happen to me." You can no longer bet that the odds are in your favor; the odds have already beaten you. As a widow you hold this awareness in tandem with the knowledge that our lives are in God's hands. Because God is sovereign, you know that the odds have nothing to do with the circumstances of your life. Yet you play the odds game in your head, even as you tell yourself that God—not fate—is in control.

How can we trust God when we've been dealt a death blow? It's not easy. I have found that it helps to keep going back to God, reading his Word, praying, waiting in his presence. When I do, he gives grace and peace to carry me through the pain. He'll do the same for you.

> *Trust in the* LORD *with all your heart*
> *and lean not on your own understanding;*
> *in all your ways acknowledge him,*
> *and he will make your paths straight.*

PROVERBS 3:5-6

"What If My Husband Didn't Believe in Jesus?"

No matter what a person's belief has been in life, we cannot know what happens between him and God in those very final moments before death. We are not to judge. All we can do is tell others the reason for the hope we have. An unbelieving husband may very well experience a change of heart and an encounter with the living God that remains unknown to us this side of heaven.

The biblical example that holds hope for our loved one is the story of the thief on the cross. Hanging there, close to death, this man said, "'Jesus, remember me when you come into your kingdom.' [And] Jesus answered him, 'I tell you the truth, today you will be with me in paradise'" (Luke 23:42-43). This private moment between Jesus and the man offers comfort when a loved one's faith is in question.

"Where Can I Find Comfort?"

LET YOURSELF CRY

Some days a good, hard cry brings healing to the soul. It is cleansing and wonderfully freeing.

When I needed to cry, my bathtub was my "dissolving spot." I'd wait till the girls were asleep, and then I'd retreat behind two doors and a hallway. I'd fill the tub with almost-scalding water, light candles, and put a tape of torch songs in the cassette player. As the melancholy music brought haunting memories of Jack and me in our younger days, I'd weep until I was spent. My soul ached with longing for what would never be again. My tears mixed with beads of sweat that drenched my face, soaking me with grief.

Then relief would come flooding in, overtaking the pain that had pierced me. I'd let my shoulders sink down into the water as I breathed in the comforting vapors of the steam and scented candles. God filled my heart with his peace.

God's comfort is mysterious and miraculous. It certainly can't be explained. How is it possible to be comforted when you've lost a loved one? God's touch transcends human reason. Somehow he comes and washes the open wounds of our soul with his love. Could it be he, too, knows how it feels to lose the one closest to you?

Find your own dissolving spot. Choose a private place where you won't be disturbed. Go there when you feel like crying and release all your emotions. Invite God to join you and to comfort you.

> *The* LORD *is close to the brokenhearted*
> *and saves those who are crushed in spirit.*
>
> PSALM 34:18

COMFORT THROUGH A DREAM

Jack came to me one night in a dream. It was so real that I wouldn't even have thought it a dream, but I awoke and found myself in bed. Just that day I had said to someone, "I wish I could talk to Jack for five minutes, just five minutes. I just want to know if I am doing things the way he would want—things like the qualifications for the athletic award at the girls' school. I mean, it's named after him. I want it to reflect what he would want. Just five minutes."

My sympathetic listener sighed and said nothing. What was there to say? Jack would not be visiting me.

Then I dreamed he was there. I was in a car that had stopped along a deserted road. The door opened and Jack got in. He looked at me, smiled, and said, "I only have five minutes, but I just wanted to tell you that you are doing fine."

He sat and looked at me, never touching me, and I drank in the loving acceptance on his face. His hand opened the car door without his looking away from me. He stepped out of the car and closed the door. I woke up with tears streaming down my face. That was the only dream in which Jack gave me a message.

I don't believe we can communicate with the dead through mediums and séances. But God used dreams in the Old Testament to communicate with people, and I believe he can do that today if he chooses. Whether my dream was simply a dream, or more than that, I'll never know this side of heaven. But God used it to bring me hope and healing in the midst of great pain. He can do the same for you—through a dream or otherwise.

You Are on Dry Land

There were days when all kinds of disturbing thoughts swirled through my mind: *Will I ever be happy again? Will my children be forever scarred by their father's death? Will I make wise choices about finances? Will I be able to earn a living?*

On those days I had a hard time believing I would survive widowhood. I had to remind myself over and over again that my feelings were not an indication of the actual condition of my life. Intellectually I believed the promises of God, but at times I was still so afraid. I longed for peace, but sometimes I saw only a frightening future ahead.

Then a scripture came to mind that I wrote down on an index card and carried with me everywhere:

> Then Moses stretched out his hand over the sea, and all
> that night the LORD drove the sea back with a strong
> east wind and turned it into dry land. The waters were
> divided, and the Israelites went through the sea on dry

ground, with a wall of water on their right and on their left. (Exodus 14:21-22)

While crossing the Red Sea in their escape from Egypt, the children of Israel must have been terrified. Walls of water towered above them on both sides, and Pharaoh's army chased them from behind. But they walked on dry land. Not slippery mud or slowing slush. Dry land!

We, too, are on dry land. No matter what our emotions tell us, we have God's promise that we are on solid footing as long as we follow him.

"Can Our Loved Ones See Us?"

Many years after Jack's death, I was watching *Always,* a movie about loss. Holly Hunter plays Dorinda, the vivacious, young pilot whose love, Pete (played by Richard Dreyfuss), dies in a plane crash.

One particular scene touched me even though it had been years since my own loss. On a lazy, summer evening about a year after Pete's death, Dorinda slips a tape into a player and listens nostalgically to the song that she and Pete had dubbed their own. The melancholy strains of "Smoke Gets in Your Eyes" fill the room, and Dorinda begins to sway as if dancing with Pete.

Tears spilled down my cheeks as I once again experienced the physical ache of Jack's death. I watched Dorinda slow dance with her invisible partner and sobbed with the pain of absence. I missed so much about Jack! His touch. His clean-shaven cheek resting against my upturned face. His arm holding me close. His grace as a dance partner. The memories were at once wonderful and excruciating.

In the movie, the audience has an advantage over the partnerless Dorinda. We can see the ghostlike image of Pete who glides undetected around Dorinda's swaying body.

"I know you can't see me, but I can see you," Pete silently whispers.

Many widows have asked me, "Do you think our loved ones can see us?"

We certainly want them to. We imagine them present. I've had many moments when I am convinced that Jack must see what is happening in my life or in the lives of our children.

I cannot prove this theologically, but I know we are surrounded by spiritual realities that we can't see. And I also believe there are unexplainable moments when we can sense the presence of our departed loved ones.

However, living in a fantasy is unhealthy. It inhibits our ability to fully live today. So don't dally with strange spirits and illusions. Instead, allow yourself moments of mystery in the protection of God's care. If you sense the presence of a departed loved one, simply smile and be content with the realities you know.

> *No eye has seen, no ear has heard, no mind has con-*
> *ceived what God has prepared for those who love him.*
>
> 1 CORINTHIANS 2:9

YOUR HUSBAND IS SAVING YOU
A SEAT AT A BANQUET

Scripture tells us that heaven is like a wedding banquet (see Matthew 22). This particular image of heaven came to life for me one dreary, Sunday morning while I was visiting a beautiful, old stone church, designed like a European cathedral. At the front of the sanctuary a massive stained-glass window glimmered with scenes of Jesus and his disciples.

The pastor asked the congregation to look up at the window and envision it opening up and a large banquet table extending into the heavens. He went on to paint a picture of the celebration that we will be part of when we all are with the Lord. There will be no pain, no tears of sorrow. We will be at the same table with God himself, and we'll have an eternity of new life ahead of us. It was, and is, an exciting thought.

Then I saw a new heaven and a new earth, for the first heaven and the first earth had passed away, and there was no longer any sea. I saw the Holy City, the new Jerusalem, coming down out of heaven from God, prepared as a bride beautifully dressed for her husband. And I heard a loud voice from the throne saying, "Now the dwelling of God is with men, and he will live with them. They will be his people, and God himself will be with them and be their God. He will wipe every tear from their eyes. There will be no more death or mourning or crying or pain, for the old order of things has passed away." He who was seated on the throne said, "I am making everything new!" Then he

*said, "Write this down, for these words are trust-
worthy and true."*

REVELATION 21:1-5

~❧~

NEW AND GLORIOUS BODIES

I remember picturing Jack in heaven when I was asked to choose the clothes I wanted him to be buried in. Now, I believe that his soul went immediately to heaven. And Scripture tells us that we will have new bodies in heaven, so I don't know why I even worried about what was covering his earthly body. But I picked out a traditional outfit of khaki slacks, a white shirt, navy and gold tie, navy blue blazer, socks and loafers. Picturing him alive in heaven, walking around in perfectly beautiful surroundings, I felt secure that my choice would please him. Then I realized that I had forgotten to include a belt. I felt terrible. Jack was a meticulous dresser and would never have walked around beltless.

Then I laughed at myself and my limited picture of heaven. Many aspects of heaven are shrouded behind a veil of mystery, but we are told that we will have new bodies—perfect, pain-free, and unravaged by earthly age. We'll be perfectly—gloriously!—dressed in heaven's most wondrous attire.

> *Our citizenship is in heaven. And we eagerly await*
> *a Savior from there, the Lord Jesus Christ, who, by*
> *the power that enables him to bring everything*
> *under his control, will transform our lowly bodies*
> *so that they will be like his glorious body.*
>
> PHILIPPIANS 3:20-21

OUR HUSBANDS SEE CLEARLY

We who are left behind are limited in our ability to understand God and his purposes. Our vision is blurred by this sin-tainted world. As soon as we gain one insight, another challenge pops up in front of us. But our husbands are no longer hindered by such obstructions. They are in the presence of God and enjoying the rewards of that close communion. Heaven is a place of transparency without fear—knowing and being known, accepting and being accepted, loving and being loved.

Now we see but a poor reflection as in a mirror;
then we shall see face to face. Now I know in part;
then I shall know fully, even as I am fully known.

1 Corinthians 13:12

A Place of Lasting Joy

I remember talking to my children about heaven and likening it to a long and fabulous vacation. But that description falls far short. Earthly vacations often have their share of challenges, including expense, possible illness, bad weather, missed connections, lost luggage, and always having to come back to the dailiness of life.

Not so with heaven. Perfect always and forever and ever—who can even imagine?!

My heart is glad and my tongue rejoices;
*   my body also will rest secure,*
because you will not abandon me to the grave,
*   nor will you let your Holy One see decay.*
You have made known to me the path of life;
*   you will fill me with joy in your presence,*
*   with eternal pleasures at your right hand.*

PSALM 16:9-11

A TASTE OF HEAVEN

For a number of years, Jack and I were involved in an international evangelism training program. Twice a year, pastors from all over the world gathered at Coral Ridge Presbyterian Church, Fort Lauderdale, Florida, and learned the techniques that we used year-round.

At one particular training seminar, after seven days of workshops and three nights of calling on people in the surrounding area, we ended the training with a session in the main sanctuary.

Many people had made professions of faith, and the excitement level was high.

The last thing we all did together was to form a large circle around the outside row of pews, join hands, and sing "We Are One in the Spirit." Many nations were represented. People of diverse backgrounds and cultures sang in stunning harmony. Tears of joy flowed freely down the faces of men and women; eyes were closed or looking heavenward; hands were joined and raised. It was a taste of what is to come.

> *After this I looked and there before me was a great multitude that no one could count, from every nation, tribe, people and language, standing before the throne and in front of the Lamb.*
>
> REVELATION 7:9

"Help! I Never Wanted to Be a Single Parent!"

"I'm Afraid to Discipline Too Much!"

"I'm afraid to discipline my children too much," Judy told me with tears in her eyes. "They've been through so much, I don't want to hurt them. But they are really out of hand." Children suffer the loss of a father in ways they often cannot articulate. Surging emotions pull them to and fro as their little minds and hearts absorb the impact of their loss. Because they don't have the vocabulary to express their feelings, children often voice their grief through disruptive behavior or disobedience.

And sometimes children are just being children; sometimes they push the limits to see how much they can get away with. Their behavior may be normal kid stuff and not intentionally aggressive.

When widowhood plunged me into single parenting, I dubbed myself a benevolent dictator, with the emphasis on *benevolent*. My young children didn't get to vote on many issues. They were not able to make choices that fell into the realm of adult decision-making.

Your children need you to be the chief decision-maker in your family. Kindness and firmness can go hand in hand. Never abdicate your role as parent. Children need guidance and help in learning to integrate their loss into their lives in a way that helps them grow, not to use it as an excuse for disruptive behavior.

If you are struggling in this area, talk with some parents you admire about how they lovingly discipline their children. Talk with your kids and assure them that you love them. Let them know that with God's help you are able to lead your household in an orderly and responsible fashion.

SHIELDING YOUR CHILD FROM MORE PAIN

I remember walking slowly back to the car where my little daughters stood crying after watching their father die in a fiery accident. They seemed rooted to the ground in fear as I pulled them close to me. "I don't know how," I whispered, "but I promise you that we will be okay." I was on my knees with one arm wrapped around each child. I tried to say comforting words and assure them that we would survive. But I told God in the silence of my heart, "I will never let these children suffer like this again." I said it not with anger but with deep conviction.

Of course I couldn't fulfill that vow. No one could. My daughters have been hurt many times since the death of their father. This has been particularly challenging because I so wanted—and still want—to protect them from enduring any more than they had already suffered.

If you have young children, love them and hug them. Pray that God's angels will surround them and carry them through all the painful moments of life.

> When you pass through the waters,
>   I will be with you;
> and when you pass through the rivers,
>   they will not sweep over you.
> When you walk through the fire,
>   you will not be burned;
>   the flames will not set you ablaze.
>
> ISAIAH 43:2

"That's Not How Daddy Used to Do It"

"Daddy wouldn't have done it that way!"

Those words ring in the ear of every widow who is a mother.

I used to feel guilty because I knew Jack would have done some things differently. I would try to remember things we'd talked about regarding the girls and second-guess what Jack would do if he were still alive.

Then I heard my married friends complaining of similar attempts by their children to play one parent against the other. I remembered my own ability to run between my parents to try to get my own way if one of them said no. I realized that even if Jack had lived, I would still have had to wrestle with how to do things.

Children who have lost their father can sculpt him into a perfect figure, posing him high on a golden pedestal, and they use that image to make mom feel inadequate. I finally stopped trying to live up to Jack's image and admitted the obvious: Daddy isn't here, no matter how perfect he might have been. "So, girls, you're stuck with me. What I say goes," I told them.

Let go of trying to live exactly as you would live if your husband were still alive.

Do the best you can to instill those important values that your husband wanted for your children, and trust your own ability to parent effectively on your own.

Kids Long to Be "Normal"

Lisa had been without her father for almost eight years when she headed out to California as a college freshman. She and I packed up all her belongings and unpacked them in the dorm room that she was to share with three other girls. Two sets of bunk beds, four desks and four built-in dressers and closets were adorned with all the trappings of teenage girls on their first adventure away from home. Clothes, makeup, all manner of electronic gear, and pictures. The top shelf of Lisa's desk held about a dozen framed photographs that captured special moments of her life with her family, including some of her and Jack during the last years of his life.

A few months later, I made the first of many trips to see Lisa and spend the weekend with her. I rented a car at the airport, checked hastily into my hotel, and headed for her dorm. She was waiting for me as I knocked on the door of the suite her room was in. Her room looked well lived in. I smiled at the stacks of CDs and magazines and the portable makeup cases bulging with enough cosmetics to last a decade. I stopped by the shelf of pictures and lingered on those of Jack with Lisa. "Have you told your room-mates about Daddy?" I asked, knowing she would know what I meant.

"No," she replied with no further comment.

I was so surprised. In asking the question I had fully expected her to say yes.

"Why not?"

"I just want to feel normal," she answered quietly, with no invitation to continue this discussion. I let it go, but I thought a lot about what she had said.

Lisa felt different, and perhaps stigmatized, because she came from a single-parent family. I had felt that way as a single mom, but it hadn't occurred to me that my children might also feel awkward after almost eight years.

Later that weekend, I encouraged Lisa to tell her roommates that her father had died when she was ten years old. She nodded sadly, but I knew she would manage to get it out in her own timing.

All of us—even children—need to feel "normal." Talk with

your kids about how they feel about being part of a single-parent family. Encourage them to be open with trusted friends, but don't push them. Extroverted children may open up much sooner and more often than introverted children. Allow both types of personalities to adjust at their own pace.

You Have All You Need to Be a Good Parent

In losing Jack, I lost the father of my children. My grief was compounded by theirs.

Jack and I met in high school. He was strong and self-confident, and I relied on him greatly. We made many decisions together, especially with regard to the children, but because he was very wise, I often agreed with him without hesitation. I missed his parenting insights deeply. I remember looking in the mirror and asking myself how in the world I could parent those little ones on my own.

As the days and weeks passed, I learned to cling to God's promise that he is "a father to the fatherless, a defender of widows"

(Psalm 68:5). God didn't speak to me in an audible voice or appear at the breakfast table with advice for the day. But a growing sense of self-confidence and God-reliance seeped into the parenting void that Jack used to fill.

I listened to the counsel of godly friends and read recommended articles and books. Mostly I sat with a written list in my hand before my Father and asked for his help. Over time God gave me the assurance that I could be a good mom. I hadn't felt that way even before Jack died. It felt good, freeing, to say, "I can do this."

You have all you need to be the parent God wants you to be. If you don't feel this now, bring your concerns to the Father. Talk to him, wait, cry, listen. Go about your day. Sit before him again with your questions. See what happens.

His divine power has given us everything we need
for life and godliness through our knowledge of him
who called us by his own glory and goodness.

2 PETER 1:3

"Now you have to be both mother and father to your children." The well-meaning people who said this to me were trying to offer empathy and support, and at first I took their words to heart.

But I failed.

I wasn't Jack. He was big, strong, athletic, a night person who would stay up late to play with the girls on Friday nights, a floor wrestler, an impish kid-at-heart on the playground, a male presence in their lives.

I was not and never will be my children's father, and neither will you be a father to your children. A load was lifted from my shoulders when I gave up this false expectation. I encourage you to do the same.

While it's true that no one can replace their father, your children still need men in their lives. Male family friends can sometimes stand in the gap, taking your kids to ball games or on fishing trips, teaching them how to change the oil in a car or how to mow the lawn, giving them hugs and showing interest in them personally. Teachers, coaches, pastors, youth workers, and your own family members can provide male role models for your kids.

Concentrate on being the best mother you can be and foster relationships with reliable and trustworthy family and friends—

and entrust your kids to the God who is "a father to the fatherless" (Psalm 68:5).

⁓⁂⁓

IF YOUR CHILD IS AFRAID OF THE DARK

Many young children envision perilous dangers lurking in their
closets and under their beds as soon as the bedroom lights are
turned off at night. Children who have lost a father to death face
these same fears, and unlike other children, they know that sometimes their worst fears *do* come true.

Lisa never experienced this bedtime angst, but Lara did. I
would read the Bible as I tucked Lara in under the covers. Then
we'd pray and I'd talk with her about God and his angels protecting
her. But no matter what our routine was, she was still afraid of the
dark. I put a night-light in her room, but the light was too dim for
comfort. Lara couldn't fall asleep unless the overhead light was on.

I talked and cajoled and tried to convince her to sleep with the
light off. Nothing worked. Then one day I asked myself what was
the big deal anyway. What was so damaging about just letting her

sleep with the light on? I decided that relieving Lara's fear was far more important.

I left the light on, and she fell asleep peacefully. Later that evening I turned off the overhead light and switched on the night-light. Lara gradually began to use the night-light instead of the overhead light. She eventually became a sleeper who preferred no light at all.

Some of your children's fears will be difficult to relieve. Fear of the dark, however, is easily remedied. Your pediatrician or family doctor will also be able to give you suggestions on how to help your child sleep peacefully.

YOUR CHILD'S FEAR OF YOUR DEATH

Children who have lost their father are usually afraid they will also lose their mother. Even though this is normal, it can be very disturbing for children.

When Lara and Lisa began expressing their fear that I might die too, I decided to have them talk with a counselor. My older daughter, Lisa, resisted, consistent with her introverted nature, but I sent both of them anyway.

I spoke with the counselor first and told him about Jack's death and that the girls were afraid of losing me as well. He assured me that he would not gloss over the issue but would talk directly with them about what would happen to them if I did die. This sounded scary, but I knew it was for their best. The girls and I had already talked about the couple who would be their guardians if something happened to me. They loved this couple and knew they would be cared for and loved.

After the counseling session, Lisa and Lara said little about what had transpired. The counselor told me privately that they had talked openly and had listened carefully to him as he reviewed with them how well they would be cared for in the event of my death. Tough stuff. But such a discussion addressed their fear of abandonment. They still struggled, but both girls seemed less anxious and more able to let me out of their sight without extreme fear.

If you have kids, don't put off making arrangements for their care in the event of your own death. Be sure you have an updated will that covers all eventualities, including guardianship. Talk with your children about how loved and cared for they would be. Then don't dwell on fearful issues, but draw their attention to the present, to your love and commitment to them, and to their heavenly

Father's even greater love. If your children's fear is unrelieved by these discussions, don't hesitate to send them to a counselor.

PUTTING FIRST THINGS FIRST

"My friends keep encouraging me to have an active social life," Anne told me. She had been a widow for about a year. "They think I am neglecting myself and that I'll never meet any men who might be potential husbands. The trouble is, I am so tired and my kids seem to resent my being out too often at night."

I'd had similar conversations during the years when I spent almost every weekend night and several weeknights in gymnasiums watching my girls play volleyball and basketball. "You'll never get remarried if you are always with your kids," lamented one assertive matchmaker.

Well-meaning people sometimes put pressure on widows to be socially active and eventually remarry. They believe that remarriage is the goal of every widowed woman. Most widows I know do want to remarry someday, but putting your social life ahead of your children's needs is a mistake.

When my children were still in elementary school, a Friday or Saturday social event didn't interfere with their schedule. But as soon as Lisa entered junior high, all that changed. She became involved in sports, and our evenings filled up with one event after another. A few years later, Lara began a similar routine. Between practices, games, and tournaments, I had little time for other activities.

And I loved it. I decided to be at *all* their games: home and away games, weeknights and weekend nights. Once the decision was made, it was easy. Not everyone understood my commitment, and some frowned at my seemingly unbalanced life. One man invited me to a Christmas party that happened to be on the same night as one of the girl's basketball games. When I declined his invitation, he was aghast that I would choose to miss a once-a-year party for a game that was played several times a week.

I am not suggesting that you make the same sweeping decision as I did. I enjoy sports and wouldn't have wanted to be elsewhere. You may not feel the same and making such a commitment would be more of a sacrifice. You might decide to have one night out a week for yourself or to devote certain evenings to be with your children and leave other nights open for negotiation. Whatever you decide, I am recommending that you communicate to your children that they come before your social life, and then stick to that decision.

The investment you make in the lives of your children will be worth the effort. Kids need both quality time *and* quantity time. You also need time with other adults and entertainment that refreshes you, but strive for a balance that gives your children the comfort and assurance that they are your first priority.

"I Can't Remember What Daddy Looked Like"

By the time Lara was a junior in high school, her father had been gone for nine years. She spoke of him often and adorned her room with pictures of them together.

During one particular week that year, I noticed that she was sitting on her bed every night, slowly leafing through the pages of a photo album and crying softly. The album was one that I had made for each of the girls. Many of the pictures were eight-by-ten-inch school photos of Jack from high school and college. The pages bulged with action shots and newspaper clippings. I didn't interrupt Lara, knowing she was just remembering her dad and feeling sad that he wasn't alive to see her play basketball.

After a week of the same scenario each night, I went in and sat on the edge of her bed.

"What are you doing honey?" I asked softly.

Looking up through tears she said, "I can't remember what Daddy looks like. Every night I stare at these pictures and try to remember, but then I just can't."

I hugged her, and we cried together. Then I took the album and gently closed it. "You don't have to remember," I told her. "You will be with Daddy again. For now, enjoy the pictures and the memories that you do have, and stop worrying about seeing him in your mind. Daddy will always live in your heart, and he is alive right now in heaven."

She smiled and wiped her tears.

Once-clear memories eventually fade from our minds and our children's minds, and we need not struggle to hang on to them. Assure your children that a dimmed memory is not a disloyalty. Even though their memories have faded, their love for their dad will live in their hearts forever.

You and your children will always remember the anniversary of your husband's death. While this is not an anniversary to be celebrated, it is important to acknowledge your loss.

My daughters and I never established a ritual that we repeated every year. Sometimes we did something together that their dad would have enjoyed; sometimes we had a special meal together after school; sometimes we exchanged notes and a few spoken words.

When we became separated geographically, I started to remember the day in a simple way that I have continued, even though we now live close together again. I send each of my girls a dozen roses every December 15 with a card that says, "Remembering. Love, Mom."

As the years pass, your way of remembering the anniversary of your husband's death will change and evolve. Do whatever seems most meaningful and comforting for you and your children. Sometimes less is more, and your children will prefer to experience this day without much outward expression. It doesn't mean they don't remember or feel deeply.

Losing Your Husband When Your Children Are Grown

Nina was in her early fifties when her husband died. Her three children were grown and living away from her home. "They were a tremendous support when Ron died," she said. "But now they have trouble treating me like an adult. They're hovering and constantly checking up on me. I appreciate their concern, but I am a big girl."

Nina's sentiments echo those of many widows with adult children. They love and appreciate their children and their concern, but they struggle with developing a balance in their relationship that allows them to retain their independence while allowing their children to offer comfort and support.

Not all women are like Nina. Some respond in an opposite way, becoming more and more dependent on their adult children. If they begin to rely too heavily on their children, this can strain the relationship.

If your children are adults, give them time to adjust to the loss of their father and the implications of that on their relationship with you. Allow them time and space to help you. But if their enthusiasm becomes intrusive, gently and lovingly talk with them about the ways you would like for them to engage with you. Schedule times to have them over or to go out with them. Communicate with them about ways you are managing well and are feeling good about yourself for being able to handle new things. Thank them for their concern and offers of help, but be specific about what you want to take care of on your own and what you would appreciate help on.

But if you are relying on your kids to take care of nearly all of your needs—asking them to accompany you or to drive you to appointments when you can drive yourself, calling them and crying on the phone after the first few weeks, planning most of your social events with them instead of with friends your age—you will need to become more responsible for yourself. If you know you are doing this or are unsure whether you are, talk with your children and ask them to be honest with you. Don't get angry or defensive if they express frustration with your reliance on them. Take that information and use it to make changes. Cultivate friendships, join groups at your church, go to a grief workshop, talk with existing friends. You will feel much better for it.

If your adult children are not helpful, grieve that loss and initiate interaction with them. If they still don't respond, back off and entrust them to God. Usually, adult children respond to you in much the same way they always have. If you were distant from them before your husband's death, that distance may remain afterward.

❧

The Widow Without Children

If you and your husband had hoped to have children, your loss will be compounded by the death of this dream. The childless widows I've met who wanted children express a deep sadness that they don't have the physical extension of their husband living on in his children. They are missing what never came to be and will never be in the future. They may remarry and have children, but they will not see the imprint of their first husband on any of those little ones.

Give yourself time to grieve for what did not happen. Go before God and cry out your pain to him. Ask him to heal this aspect of your journey through widowhood just as you ask him to heal all other painful portions of your heart.

"Who Provides the Spiritual Direction for My Children?"

I was speaking about single parenting at a conference on the East Coast a few years ago. One of my points was that children in single-mother homes need spiritual direction, and the mother is primarily responsible for that teaching.

A hand shot up from the back of the room, and a man called out to get my attention. He stood up and began to tell me that I was not speaking scripturally. He said that it was the responsibility of the church to provide male leadership for single women and their children. I asked him if his church provided such a service, and he murmured, "No," and quickly sat down.

God says that he is the father to the fatherless and the defender of widows, and that there is one mediator between man and God, Jesus Christ. Single mothers who know Jesus personally have direct access to him, his guidance, and his help.

Your church may teach male leadership in the home, but know that as a single mom you have the responsibility and the spiritual resources to be that leader in the absence of your husband. You are now responsible for teaching your children spiritual truths. Trust God to give you wisdom and insight as you seek to mold and shape your children's hearts toward him.

Perhaps you married when you were past the age of having children, or maybe you and your husband chose not to have children. You are not grieving a loss that did not occur, but you are grieving the loss of your spouse without the comfort that children bring. You may not have family calling to check on you or invite you to join them for social times.

It's important not to succumb to isolation. Maintain friendships or, if friends seem few and far between, try to cultivate new ones. This can be done in the context of grieving if you join a grief workshop or widows' group. Couples are healthy companions too. Don't cut yourself off. Be around others. It will help you heal.

A father to the fatherless, a defender of widows, is
God in his holy dwelling.

PSALM 68:5

"How Do I Deal with Other People?"

———

Soak in the Love

In the weeks after Jack's death, friends and family stepped in and took over many of my daily tasks. People took turns cleaning the house and cooking all our meals. A friend picked up our laundry and returned it, clean and neatly folded. A man from our church came every week and cut the grass. These acts of love allowed me time to get through the difficult days of adjustment and added responsibility.

I called a friend from the scene of Jack's accident, and she was at our house by the time I got home. She handled the continuous phone calls. That evening I asked her to stay with the girls and me for the first few weeks, just to help me get through the days. As we talked for hours on end, she became my lifeline. The weeks turned into a month, and I asked my friend to stay on indefinitely. She agreed. This dear friend lived with us for two years. During that time, I was on the receiving end of a friendship that has lasted and grown to this day.

In the early days of your loss, graciously accept help. When healing has strengthened you, you will begin to give again. For now, soak in the love others want to shower on you and your family.

When Everyone Has an Opinion

My mother was appalled that I never put flowers on Jack's grave. She thought it was disrespectful, and she worried that other people would think I didn't miss him. I explained to her that I didn't think of Jack as being in that grave, and that he would have wanted me to spend that money for something other than graveside flowers.

My mother died almost nine years ago, and every Christmas and Easter I order a large floral arrangement for her grave. Does that seem inconsistent? I want to respect both my husband and my mother in a manner that they would have wished. I care much more about what mattered to those two people I loved very much than about what other people may think about my actions.

You will have to make myriad choices: legal, financial, business, personal, spiritual, and parental, from the buying and selling of property to the accessories you want on your next car. Some of these decisions will come easily, and you will feel confident about your choices. Others will cause sleepless nights and anxious nail biting.

In the days ahead, you will receive all kinds of advice—some good, some bad. Pray for discernment and seek godly counsel. In small issues, learn to make the decisions and then relax. In big issues, draw on the wisdom of others whom you can trust. Talk to God about what choices to make.

"No One Mentions His Name"

For a few weeks after Jack's memorial service, my friends and I talked of nothing else but him. We laughed and cried and looked at pictures. Our reminiscing helped ease the pain caused by the wrenching away of a life so entwined with ours.

Then, with the exception of a few people, people stopped talking about Jack. There was an unspoken decision to move on. I felt as if everyone had simply buried the memory with the man. Others had told me this would happen, but I still wasn't prepared. I wanted to keep talking because talking meant remembering. I wanted to say Jack's name out loud, over and over. *Jack, Jack, Jack!* Saying his name helped me remember all that he was to me, and it hurt me that others seemed uncomfortable talking about him.

I know now that silence from others doesn't mean callousness or lack of feeling. It is one of the ways that people deal with grief. Eventually I grew more comfortable with other's discomfort about mentioning even the name of my husband around me. You will too.

"Why Don't You Cry?"

I was walking into church one Sunday morning when a woman came up to me, grabbed me by the shoulders, and shook me. "Why don't you cry?" she demanded. I was so startled I didn't say a word. She let go of me and walked off in exasperation. *Wow*, I thought to myself, *she's really upset with me.*

People express grief in deeply personal ways. Some weep openly and often. Others, like me, don't reveal their deepest feelings much in public.

All of us look at others and draw conclusions from their actions or lack of action; we assume, conclude, judge. It's helpful to realize other people do the same to us. I don't think their motives are any more suspect than mine are. They don't mean to be hurtful. In fact, much of the time their conclusions reflect where they are rather than where they think we are.

Forgive those who unintentionally hurt you by evaluating your grief and telling you how you should be responding. Forgive them and then grieve in your own way.

SOUL FRIENDS

In those early days of grief—and the days since—three women faithfully and unconditionally accepted and supported me. Many others touched and comforted me in a multitude of ways, but those three are soul friends.

Soul friends know all about you and love you anyway. They have the patience to walk with you through dark times, times when it would be easier to leave you to your own misery. Soul friends are with you for the long haul. They are burden bearers. These saints are at your side in a hospital, at a grave, and on many a lonely night in the years after you're widowed.

These supporters make a huge difference in the lives of widows, and they pay a heavy price. They give of their time, their emotion, their energy. They experience personal pain on your behalf. Thank God for them. Remember them. As you grow stronger, let them know how grateful you are for them.

FEWER CLOSE RELATIONSHIPS

Any schedule I had maintained before Jack's death was nowhere to be found afterward. My life was turned upside down. He wasn't there to drive the kids to school or to pick up bread on the way home from the office. He wasn't there to fix the stopped-up toilet or to mow the lawn. He wasn't there to balance our checkbook or to pay the monthly bills.

All the details of our lives now fell to me. The added responsibilities consumed my time and energy. I didn't anticipate how this would impact my friendships, but it resulted in the slow and unintentional end to some. I had little regular contact with many women I had previously seen often. And because I was single, I wasn't invited to as many social events by some couples Jack and I had known in the past.

It is still sometimes painful for me to look at old pictures and see people with whom I was once close. They were an important part of my life. But my priorities changed, and I had to let go.

You may need to do the same. You may feel exhausted, unable to keep up some of your former contacts. Do what you can and graciously let go of those relationships that begin to dwindle. Some people will be in your life no matter what, and others will fade. People move in and out of our lives, but God stays forever.

> *And surely I am with you always, to the very end of the age.*
>
> MATTHEW 28:20

101

Recognizing Other People's Pain

On December 15, 1998, nineteen years after Jack's death, I picked up the phone to hear a young man's voice. It was Jimmy (he now goes by James, but he'll always be Jimmy to me), the son of dear friends—one of those couples who are in our lives forever. When Jimmy was in high school, he was close to Jack. Jack and I traveled around south Florida and enthusiastically cheered Jimmy on in his basketball successes. Our families were often at each other's homes and enjoyed many rich times together.

When Jack died, Jimmy was away at college. He came home for the memorial service and was obviously upset and shocked by this sudden loss. Just two days after Jack's accident, Jimmy received a letter from Jack. It had been written and mailed the day before the accident. It was just a note to say hi, and to encourage Jimmy in his current pursuits. That letter is now framed and has hung on a wall of Jimmy's home ever since.

I am often in touch with Jimmy's parents, but have spoken with him less frequently as the years have passed. So I was surprised to hear his voice on the phone last December.

"Hi, Lois," he said tentatively.

"Hi, Jimmy!"

"I just called…," he stammered. He couldn't finish and was choking back audible sobs. Jimmy hung up, and I sat in stunned silence. The depth of his pain so many years later moved me deeply.

A few minutes later the phone rang again, and Jimmy's mother was on the line. Jimmy had called her to explain what he had tried to do but couldn't quite complete. He had asked her to call me and explain because he didn't think he could get out the words to me personally.

Of course, I knew. He had called to tell me he remembered. He remembered Jack and that day so long ago, and that December 15 marked another anniversary. Marian and I talked and cried a little and shared the bittersweet communion of those who have suffered a common loss.

When we lose a spouse, we and our children receive most of the comfort and concern. But others suffer, too. Remember their pain and pray God will comfort them as well.

PART II

WHEN YOU'RE
READY TO
MOVE AHEAD

"How Do I Move on with My Life?"

PUTTING AWAY THE PHOTOS

One day, several years after Jack's death, I looked around and saw my home in a new light. Jack's photographs seemed oddly out of place. I realized that I pictured him having a wonderful time in heaven much more than I thought about him as he was captured in the photos.

At first the thought of removing those photographs seemed disloyal. Would people think that I had forgotten him? That I didn't want to be reminded of him? Those voices nagged me for a few days. Then I decided to talk with Lisa and Lara and tell them why I was going to change many of the photos: It was time to focus on our lives in the present and the future.

They understood, and we lovingly stored the visual account of their dad's life.

Cleaning Out the Closet

One of the most painful tasks a widow performs is removing her husband's personal belongings from their bedroom: his clothes from the closet and dresser, the clutter of items he kept on the bureau, the stack of magazines next to his side of the bed. It's as if each item carries the traces of conversations and imprints of moments you experienced together, including your most intimate moments.

Many widows put off this task for months. But the day will come when you will be ready to let go and make the bedroom your own. When is up to you. It took me many months.

There's a cowboy in Davie, Florida (yes, Florida does have cowboys!), wearing a T-shirt with my picture on it, a photographic image imprinted on a yellow shirt that Jack had proudly worn when cutting the grass or shooting hoops in the driveway. That shirt was swept into one of the boxes that contained most of Jack's clothes. I had left his side of our closet untouched for many months after his death. I couldn't face another empty half. I already had so many: his side of the car, his side of the bed, his chair at the table, his end of the couch, his place in the pew, his voice on the other end of the phone, his active presence in all parts of my heart.

So I avoided removing his clothes from his side of our walk-in closet. Then one day in May, I asked a friend to come over and help me take away the most personal of his belongings. I buried my face in his shirts and inhaled deeply. His scent still lingered, evoking sweet memories. Grief welled up inside me, and tears flowed, releasing pain from somewhere deep inside.

My friend and I sorted through each memory-laden item, saving a few basketball jerseys, an army flight jacket, and his graduation cap and gown. I stacked his T-shirts without looking at each one. Later I realized, with a smile, that the one with my photo was among the bunch.

I watched out the window as my friend's car headed off to Davie to donate the clothing to a charity. Then I sat in the closet and cried.

Whether with a friend, a family member, or alone, clean out the closet. Choose your own time, but face the pain.

I became a widow at thirty-four. I was young and dependent and naive about the world, although I didn't think so at the time. In our marriage I had seldom expressed a contrary opinion and was content to follow Jack's lead.

Then he was gone. Aspects of my personality began to emerge, aspects I hadn't known were there. I could be assertive when I needed to be; I could disagree graciously but firmly; I could make decisions that I'd never made before. It felt good.

Undoubtedly some of those changes would have come whether I had been widowed or not. But widowhood forces rapid change. And change brings with it a need to grieve and to rejoice— to grieve the loss of the old you and to rejoice at the birth of the new you.

Don't insist on remaining the same person you were. Recognize that even if your husband had lived, your perspectives and preferences would change. Allow yourself to become excited about how God will change and refine you. He can bring you joy that you never thought possible.

One of my good friends was widowed before I knew her. She is a spunky, outspoken, vivacious woman. She writes and speaks and travels and amazes her children and friends at the woman she has become. I am told that before her husband died, she was the same sweet person she is today, but she was painfully shy and retiring. She lived in her outgoing husband's shadow, and many expected that she would shrivel up and withdraw from life when he died.

She certainly didn't withdraw. She grew and changed and lives life fully.

You can too.

TAKING RISKS

Jack and I had lived in Florida for almost ten years when he was killed. I had intended to stay there for the rest of my life. But as the girls and I adjusted to life without him, we grew restless. While I knew it wasn't good to make big decisions during the first year of widowhood, by the time three years had passed, we began to consider a move across the country.

I visited a friend who lived in Colorado Springs, Colorado. Some of my friends thought I had lost my mind to even consider moving there. But for us it seemed right. I prayed and waited and talked with others for input. After a thoughtful process, I decided to take the risk and move.

It was a wonderful adventure for the girls and me, and it began a new phase of our lives. Not all risks are as dramatic as moving across country, but it is fun and exciting to begin to ask God to show you where he wants you to spread your wings.

BECOMING WONDER WOMAN

When the girls and I moved from Fort Lauderdale to Colorado Springs, we acquired a new family member: Heidi, a Siberian husky whose wintry look and wild spirit fit our new home. One morning I got up before Lisa and Lara and went downstairs to make my daily pot of coffee. I let Heidi outside and watched her run back and forth on our deck, sniffing the cool air and surveying her domain. I busied myself with the coffee making and wandered leisurely into the family room with my first steaming cup of the day.

Heidi was standing outside the back door with her face close to the doorknob. I automatically went over and let her in. She jaunted proudly past me, then turned around to display the bird that was crunched between her teeth.

I started screaming and pushed her outside. Her eyes, one blue and one brown, looked perplexed as she bit down on her prize. I stood watching and screaming as she swallowed every last feather of her captured prisoner.

"Oh no!" I cried out, wondering what awful disease she might get from eating a wild bird. I ran to the phone and called our veterinarian, only to get a recorded message of who to call for an emergency. Since it was certainly an emergency to me, I called the number and explained my dilemma. The woman who answered told me to pour hydrogen peroxide down Heidi's throat to induce vomiting.

I ran upstairs and rifled through the medicine closet, relieved to find an old bottle of hydrogen peroxide. I grabbed it and ran back downstairs. Reluctantly, I let Heidi inside and approached her. She wagged her tail and pranced a little, anticipating some playtime. I tried to grab her, but she liked our game of catch-me-if-you-can and managed to avoid my clutches. "Lisa!" I yelled. "Lisa! Get down here. Hurry, I need you," I continued to yell. Lisa came running, as she struggled to open her eyes. "Heidi ate a bird," I told her in rushed tones. "We have to get this hydrogen peroxide down her throat. Help me grab her and get her mouth open."

Lisa sprang into action, and we soon had our unsuspecting

prey in hand. I poured the liquid down her throat, and we pushed her out the door. Just as Lisa and I heaved sighs of relief, Heidi threw up the bird parts, but then she began to eat them again! With the verse about dogs returning to their vomit flitting through my mind, I ran outside and tried to shoo her away from her disgusting treasure. She finally retreated. I got a bucket of hot water and a broom and swept the morning's remains off the deck. By that time, I was in tears. "No one should have to do this," I said out loud.

But I did have to do it—and somehow I survived.

When I tell this story now, I can laugh about it. But it was not funny at the time. In the days ahead, you will find that you are able to do far more than you ever dreamed.

LEAVING ON A JET PLANE

"I never traveled before, but now I am on the go all the time!" Sybil said. In her late sixties when her husband died, Sybil had never been anywhere without him. Every year for over forty years they had taken a short summer vacation to the same beach resort.

Now Sybil has discovered the world of travel. She met her traveling buddies at a church group for widows. A few of the women who were seasoned travelers suggested they all take a trip together. Everyone had a ball. Between trips they enjoy getting together, taking classes, and supporting each other when difficulties strike.

When we lose a mate, we lose a lifestyle. We no longer have a ready companion for vacations or Friday nights; we experience a void that is difficult to fill. Even though you will never fill that hole in exactly the same way, you can branch out and develop new friendships and new endeavors. Female friendships can enrich your life by encouraging you to change and grow.

Moving Beyond Labels

A friend came with me to a ladies' Bible study where I was to speak on singleness. After we introduced ourselves, we enjoyed easy small talk and delicious food for about a half-hour. Then we moved to the living room and pulled the chairs into a circle. The leader, who was the only married woman in the group, called us to order and opened with prayer. Then she asked us to go around the circle and say our names and "status."

My friend and I glanced at each other, and I asked the leader what she meant by "status."

She said, "Oh, you know, are you widowed, divorced, or never-married." I felt a shiver run up my spine and avoided making eye contact with my friend. Each woman said her name and then added the appropriate label in a resigned tone. I felt sad. The life of the single adult is often alien and isolated, and labels such as "divorced," "widowed," or "never-married" often intensify these feelings.

People are not defined by their marital status. It is simply one of the many facts about a person. Move beyond such labels and recognize the unique and significant place you occupy in the kingdom and in the heart of God.

※

Celebrate Holidays in New Ways

Our first Christmas without Jack was just ten days after his accident. I decided to cook dinner at home and have my parents over. This was how we had always celebrated Christmas, so we did it again. The next Christmas was similar, a mix of joy and sadness. Memories of happier days brought tears, blurring our vision all day long.

The third year we broke our pattern and had one of the best holidays ever. A close friend was living and working in Amsterdam at the time and had invited us to come over. At first I said no because I couldn't imagine not being home for Christmas. Then the more I thought about it, the more I liked the idea of celebrating in a new way.

Since our trip was our gift to each other, the girls and I boarded our plane bound for Amsterdam with no wrapped presents. Our hearts were light, and we were excited to soon see our friend. For the next two weeks, we traveled by train throughout Germany and Austria. It was cold and snowy, and we loved it. On Christmas Eve day, we all agreed to buy one small gift for each other to put under our three-foot tree that was lighted with real candles. It was a simple and enchanting Christmas.

Christmas isn't the only holiday that will be difficult, especially during the first year of loss. All holidays can be painful. There are birthdays, anniversaries, Mother's Day and Father's Day, and other days that are special to your family. One woman I know finds Memorial Day, the Fourth of July, and Labor Day difficult because her husband loved to host large barbecues on those days. To have parties on those holidays painfully reminds her of his absence, so now she takes her children away on those weekends or accepts invitations from friends to go to their homes.

Keep those traditions you feel comfortable with, and begin new ones that will enhance your life.

"What About Men?"

―――――

WHISPERED QUESTIONS

I have met with many widows over a cup of coffee. Almost always I'm asked about dating. Many widows fear that they are feeling things they should not feel. They worry that they would be scorned if anyone really knew what they were thinking. And so they risk asking one who has been where they now sit.

Here's what they want to know:

Should I feel guilty for having sexual desires?
No, sexual desires are normal.

I think a lot about a married man I know. What should I do?
Recognize your loneliness and vulnerability and the natural-ness of your attachment to him. Don't be alone with him. Make a deliberate decision to turn your thoughts to something else when he comes into your mind. Accept that this temptation may be a

struggle, but make no moves in his direction and don't tell him you are attracted to him.

Some of my married women friends act strange when I am around. What is going on?

They may feel insecure and threatened by your presence around their husbands. Try to focus on them and don't, in any way, flirt with their husbands. Their strangeness may be due to their own insecurity and have little to do with you, but be sure your actions don't feed their fears.

A male married friend (pastor, leader at church, counselor) frequently calls me late in the evening and talks for a long time. Is this okay?

If his conversations with you are a secret, this is a red flag. Protect yourself and end the phone calls. If you don't answer his calls—get caller ID on your phone—he should get the message.

Some of these suggestions may sound overly cautious, but the number of widows who become involved in inappropriate ways is greater than many people think. While I am not aware of any statistics to support this statement, I can say that I am continually surprised at the number of women who tell me their stories when I am speaking at conferences. Just when I think I am with a group where this wouldn't be true, woman after woman comes to privately ask about her relationship with a married man.

Having said all of that, let me also say that if you set clear limits and boundaries for your relationships with men, you can enjoy wonderful friendships with married friends and single men.

When You Are Content to Stay Single

Remarriage is far from the mind of most new widows, but as time passes and healing comes, the idea of another partner often comes alive. But not always. Some women are genuinely content to remain single. They experience wholeness and fullness of life as single women and feel no desire or need to have a man in their lives. If you are one of these women, relax in your choice and fend off your well-meaning friends who try to be matchmakers.

It is often difficult for other people to understand why someone would want to remain alone, but your contentment might win them over in time.

Admitting Desire

Do you want to get married again? If so, you're not being disloyal to your husband by admitting it, so don't feel guilty.

Like most widows, I thought I would never want to remarry. But two years after Jack's death, I admitted to myself that I would like to get married again. I was never a loner, and I missed the companionship of one special man in my life. And I've always been a romantic. I longed to be part of a couple. I wanted to go through life with someone else and experience the intimacy that a spouse offers.

When I speak at singles' conferences, women often voluntarily tell me—repeatedly and loudly—that they don't want to date or remarry. But their behavior sends a different message. Such emphatic protestation usually is an attempt to deny a desire that we are afraid to face. Women who are truly content to be single typically don't broadcast that fact. They are busy living their lives and are not defensive about their singleness.

Being single or being married are equally acceptable choices. But you need to be honest with yourself and others about your true feelings—it's essential for navigating the rough waters of male-female relationships.

⌘

Vulnerability Can Lead to Poor Choices

When I was single, people used to tell me, "You are in a vulnerable position when it comes to relating to men."

"I know," I would reply.

But I didn't. Oh, I theoretically understood that loneliness influenced my thinking, but I never thought I would be tempted to become involved with men in any ungodly or unwise way. Then the months of singleness dragged into years, and my loneliness intensified. I found myself surrounded by married men, with few single men in sight. I began to accept the conclusion that statistics support: The odds of my remarrying were decreasing with every passing year.

Temptation simmered around and within the community of believers. I recognized my own undeclared emotional attachments to some of the married men around me, and I was stunned to admit that the ground on which I stood was more shaky than I had ever imagined.

Our culture's acceptance of morally compromising relationships has seeped through the walls of the church. Believers are buying the lie that we can follow Christ and at the same time be involved in affairs of the heart that do not honor God.

So be careful—careful of your feelings and rationalizations, of the compromises of others, of the influence of the culture, of your loneliness. We live in a world that provides loopholes for justifying all kinds of ungodly thinking and behavior, even inside the Christian community.

THE PAIN OF COMPROMISE

After the publication of my first book, *The Snare: Understanding Emotional and Sexual Entanglements,* I began to receive anonymous telephone calls from readers asking for help. Usually the callers were single women who had become involved with married men. These women, well beyond early temptations, were in deep pain when they called for help.

I listened to many stories of unintended compromise. While the names and specifics changed, the plot remained the same: pain of loneliness, kindness from a married man, seemingly innocent involvement, first physical involvement, relief from pain and continuance of contact, onset of guilt, and return of even greater pain than originally experienced.

Loneliness can drive us to make choices we never thought we would make. Involvement with an unavailable man is always the wrong solution, and it leads to pain compounded by guilt. With the help of the Holy Spirit and others who are committed to the same thing, choose to live by obedience. Grieve for those who stop struggling and give in to temptation. You *can* live as God desires. Keep in mind that supernatural resources are at your disposal.

> *Flee from sexual immorality. All other sins a man commits are outside his body, but he who sins sexually sins against his own body.*
>
> 1 CORINTHIANS 6:18

Avoid Romanticizing Love and Dating

As a teenager I loved to pull a big, overstuffed chair up to the television and watch late-night movies. The black-and-white images leaped to life for me most Friday or Saturday nights after coming home from high-school games or gatherings. Handsome leading men wooed beautiful damsels with flattery and passionate kisses. The qualities of fidelity, commitment, and undying love drenched me with a romanticized view of love and relationships that I took with me into the world of adult dating.

I remember getting ready for my first date as a thirty-six-year-old single adult. I felt much the same as I had at age sixteen. I spent several hours primping, beginning with a long, steamy bubble bath. I dreamily pictured the upcoming evening as I soaked amid the bubbles. I just knew this first date would be a wonderful, romantic moment that would lead to other wonderfully romantic moments. But it wasn't romantic; it was far from my expectations, and I was disappointed.

When you finally feel ready to date, be realistic about what lies ahead. Adult dating is a minefield of explosives that can throw the most pragmatic woman off her feet. Balance your excitement and anticipation with a wariness about this unfamiliar terrain.

Be aware that most adults, yourself included, have a lot of baggage when they start dating again. When you meet someone, don't make decisions too quickly, either positively or negatively. Remember, it takes time to get to know someone and to understand the implications of their past on their present. While love at first sight may sound enticing, it can be risky. Proceed with caution.

The Rules Have Changed

As a married woman, you lived with few sexual restraints beyond monogamy. Now you find yourself single again, and you are once again called to celibacy. But the rules of dating have most likely changed during the years you were married. If you are naive, you may be caught unawares and make choices you later regret. Powerful emotions that were only emerging in youth or were freely expressed in marriage can seize the most rational woman and move her into a temptation with consequences far beyond those she has confronted before. Your firm convictions about sexual morality may waiver in the seductive breeze of passion.

Be wise and wary. Adult dating is far different from teenage dating. Years of marriage removed you from the need to restrict expression of your sexual feelings. Make a decision about your level of physical involvement—and stick to it.

LET GO OF COMPARISONS

When I started dating again, I couldn't help but compare every man with Jack. I had known him since high school and had been married to him for over thirteen years. One day I said to a friend, "Everyone seems so short. Where are all the tall men?"

Jack was six-foot-two, muscular, athletic, outgoing, and had blue eyes and black, curly hair. Everything about him—his looks, personality, profession, personal tastes—was well known to me. When I met someone new, I would think about Jack. No one compared well. I once heard it said that it is impossible to compete with the dead. It's true. A late husband is a tough act to follow.

Then as time went by, I found that I could care about men

who were not at all like Jack. It became a matter of comparing apples and oranges and deciding both are fine. I chose to see each man I dated for who he was and not how he compared to Jack.

I encourage you to do the same. Let go of comparisons. Meet new men with a clean slate. Be open to who God made them to be. If you stop comparing, you will be able to view men for who they are while still appreciating who your late husband was.

BLIND DATES

One weekend a friend of mine asked me to entertain a couple visiting from Europe. I met these delightful people, and we enjoyed the sights of the West while becoming acquainted with each other. Over many conversations, I mentioned the blind dates I had endured. I never once thought about our cultural differences and just rambled on about the different men my friends had introduced me to. At the end of the day, the gentleman cautiously asked, "Why do you always go out with men who are blind?" We all had a good laugh as I explained what a blind date is.

Single women often complain about friends who seem intent on trying to get them married off. But let's be honest about this: It is difficult to meet available men without the assistance of others. So if you do want to start dating again, let some trusted friends know, and be open to the risk of going on some blind dates.

Here are a few practical tips:

- Meet your date at a neutral, public location in the daytime.
- Drive your own car.
- Meet for coffee or for a designated short amount of time.
- Graciously decline another date if you don't care to meet him again.
- If you would like to see him again and he asks to see you, decide whether you want to have him come to your home.
- If you still have children at home, meet him away from your home until you know if this will be a more lasting relationship.
- If you are absolutely crazy about the man, move slowly.
- Remember that it takes time to get to know who someone really is.

Dating relationships are complex under the best of circumstances. It is wonderful to feel alive again. Your emotions zing all over the place, and your reason may take an extended vacation. New relationships may be part of God's plan for you, but there are lots of pitfalls. Be careful, prayerful, and accountable to trusted and wise friends.

THE PROBLEM OF PERCEPTIONS

"He's the most wonderful man you will ever meet," well-meaning friends often told me. But when I met this "wonderful man," I frequently found that my friends had perceived him through a glass darkly. No doubt they viewed me with equally blurred vision. Unfortunately, the result meant I spent time with men who were not a good match for me.

Jeannie told me, "My most shocking blind date was with a friend of friends of mine from church. They listed all the usual qualifications, and ended with the fact that this man was about forty-five. I was only twenty-eight at the time, but they were so eager that I agreed to meet him. I insisted on driving my own car and meeting them for lunch instead of meeting him alone for dinner. We set up a time and place.

"It was a beautiful day in southern California as I pulled into the restaurant parking lot. Spotting my friends' car, I parked next to them and got out. I couldn't believe my eyes when my friends and a man well into his fifties approached me. They excitedly introduced us, and I silently sighed at the prospect of an afternoon with a man old enough to be my father. I have no set rules about a particular age, but this man was thirty years older than I was, and I wasn't told the truth about his age. It was very disappointing."

Many of your friends would love to be the ones who find the perfect match for you. However, their enthusiasm may cloud their vision. Before agreeing to a blind date, ask a lot of questions and trust your gut reaction.

If Mr. Right Does Come Along

Just when it seems impossible, there he is.

I had been single for almost ten years before I remarried. I had all but given up hope that I'd ever walk down the wedding aisle again.

Steve and I met in church. He came up to me one day and said he had been asked by my publisher to write some press releases on a book I had written. He wondered if we could meet for lunch. I told him that my publisher had neglected to tell me anything about him!

He was sweetly persistent, so I told him to call me at home after I had a chance to call the publisher. By the time I got home from church, he had called and left a message on my answering machine. I did verify that he was hired to do the press releases; I did have lunch with him; I did marry him a little over a year later.

It happens—and it can happen to you. You are not a statistic. No matter what your age or circumstances, God may intend for you to remarry. Until then, relax and live well.

"What Does the Future Hold?"

—

FEED ON HOPE

Without hope, we perish.

As you face the future, feed your spirit by continually returning to God and his Word. Sit with him, wait on him, struggle with him, pray, read, talk with other believers. Hope.

> *Now faith is being sure of what we hope for and certain of what we do not see.*
>
> HEBREWS 11:1

> *"For I know the plans I have for you," declares the LORD, "plans to prosper you and not to harm you, plans to give you hope and a future."*
>
> JEREMIAH 29:11

*Praise be to the God and Father of our Lord Jesus
Christ! In his great mercy he has given us new birth
into a living hope through the resurrection of Jesus
Christ from the dead, and into an inheritance that
can never perish, spoil or fade—kept in heaven for
you, who through faith are shielded by God's power
until the coming of the salvation that is ready to be
revealed in the last time.*

1 PETER 1:3-5

GOD IS FAITHFUL

My two-year-old grandson, Alex, has observed some of the worshipers in the church services he attends with his parents and brother. As a result he enthusiastically runs around with his arms up in the air saying, "Al-lu-ya," his version of "Hallelujah." He grins and waves his arms with little understanding of what his gestures mean. But I think he has gotten the message. Sometimes God's blessing so fills us that our praise spills out in words and songs and gestures.

Our certainty of God's presence and his love for us can carry us through difficulties. It can also enhance our good times with the awareness that they are his gifts.

When the future looks uncertain, remember that God is faithful and will continue to bless you.

> *I know whom I have believed, and am convinced*
> *that he is able to guard what I have entrusted to*
> *him for that day.*
>
> 2 TIMOTHY 1:12

MORE SWEET THAN BITTER

"What do you have there, Justin?" I asked my five-year-old grandson.

"My treasures from my Grandpa-Jack-in-heaven," he said as he spread out cuff links, tie tacks, and army brass insignias. The familiar men's brown jewelry box was open on the dining room table in front of Justin, who was scrutinizing each piece with special care.

137

I smiled as those old mementos brought back sweet memories: the day I pinned Jack's lieutenant's bars on his uniform, the cuff links that were a much-saved-for Christmas present, the monogrammed tie tack that he wore the night he received an insurance award.

"Do you remember these, Nana?" Justin looked up at me and asked.

"Oh yes, honey," I said, dry-eyed. "I remember."

Some memories fade, but most reside forever in a safe, lovely place in your heart. As time passes, those memories will become more sweet than bitter. You will still feel a tug or wipe away a tear, but you will be smiling too.

A RICH, FULL LIFE

This past year, Steve and I were visiting his family's home in Ohio. One Sunday after church we gave his Great-aunt Mid a ride home. Aunt Mid is ninety-seven years old and has been widowed for many years. She lives by herself in a cozy one-bedroom bungalow in an assisted-living community. Her garden next to the porch lies dormant in the winter cold, but she pointed out where her plants would come to life in the spring.

As we visited with her, she showed us her latest oil paintings and the stack of novels she's reading. She speaks lovingly of family still alive and those who are gone. Aunt Mid's life is full. She is a joy to be around and a model for the kind of woman we all could be.

No matter how long we live, or how much of that time we are alone, we can still live rich, full lives.

CLING TO HIM

When Jesus is in our lives, we live, even though our bodies may die. When he's not in our lives, we die, even though our bodies may live. Whatever pain or loss or tragedy we suffer, Jesus suffers with us and helps us endure.

Jesus holds your future in his hands and his heart. Nothing, not even death, can separate you from your Father, because his Son has given you eternal life. He makes the difference between despair and hope.

Cling to him.

Always.

> *My purpose is that they may be encouraged in heart and united in love, so that they may have the full riches of complete understanding, in order that they may know the mystery of God, namely, Christ, in whom are hidden all the treasures of wisdom and knowledge.*
>
> COLOSSIANS 2:2-3

THE WONDER OF HEALING

Many years ago I hurt my knee in a skiing accident. After surgery, the pain continued for some time but lessened with every passing day. Now remnants of that accident remind me that I was badly wounded. When I exercise a lot or when the weather is particularly damp, my knee aches a little. But only a little. It is just enough to cause me to rejoice that I can walk and run and even ski. My knee is healed.

The same is true for my heart, which was dealt a near fatal blow when Jack was killed. My heart is now healed. Oh, I still feel a moment of slight pain now and then, but I can rejoice in the middle of that moment.

The healing took place at the hand of the Great Physician. Even though there are questions I cannot answer, I believe in the goodness of God. And my healing is the result of many years of trust that our God is a loving and kind God, despite the pain of loss.

God will heal you, too. In the middle of your pain, trust him for that healing and believe that it will come to pass. It *will* happen to you, if you yield to him daily. Cry out, wait, follow, cry out again, keep breathing, wait, and continue to follow. Trust, believe…no matter how you feel. One step at a time, just keep on keeping on with Jesus.

And one day you will realize that your heart is healed. You will rejoice.

The LORD *is my strength and my shield;*
my heart trusts in him, and I am helped.

My heart leaps for joy
and I will give thanks to him in song.

PSALM 28:7

❧

GOD WILL WORK THINGS
OUT FOR YOUR GOOD

I couldn't stand it when people would come up to me and spout off the familiar words of Romans 8:28: "And we know that in all things God works for the good of those who love him, who have been called according to his purpose."

I know you know what I mean.

We believe that verse, but it stings when those words are flung at us as if to snap us out of our grief. It takes time to see goodness in our lives again, and we may never understand why God allowed our husbands to die. We may not be able to answer in our own hearts just how death can demonstrate anything good.

But many months after Jack died, I could once again look at that verse and receive the comfort it holds. There is a bigger picture than the one we see at any given moment, and God is working in all the moments of our lives. Time must pass and healing must happen before we can transform our belief in God's goodness into a reality in our lives.

God is patient, and he will stay beside you as you walk from grief to joy. Right now he is working those good things out in your life. Stay close to him.

Additional Scriptures
for Comfort, Inspiration,
and Instruction

Psalm 4:8

I will lie down and sleep in peace, for you alone, O LORD, make me dwell in safety.

Psalm 16:7-11

I will praise the Lord, who counsels me; even at night my heart instructs me. I have set the Lord always before me. Because he is at my right hand, I will not be shaken. Therefore my heart is glad and my tongue rejoices; my body also will rest secure, because you will not abandon me to the grave, nor will you let your Holy One see decay. You have made known to me the path of life; you will fill me with joy in your presence, with eternal pleasures at your right hand.

Psalm 17:8

Keep me as the apple of your eye; hide me in the shadow of your wings.

Psalm 18:33

He makes my feet like the feet of a deer; he enables me to stand on the heights.

Psalm 20:7

Some trust in chariots and some in horses, but we trust in the name of the LORD our God.

Psalm 27:8

My heart says of you, "Seek his face!" Your face, LORD, I will seek.

Psalm 27:13-14

I am still confident of this: I will see the goodness of the LORD in the land of the living. Wait for the LORD; be strong and take heart and wait for the LORD.

Psalm 28:7

The LORD is my strength and my shield; my heart trusts in him, and I am helped. My heart leaps for joy and I will give thanks to him in song.

Psalm 30:2

O LORD my God, I called to you for help and you healed me.

Psalm 30:11-12

You turned my wailing into dancing; you removed my sackcloth and clothed me with joy, that my heart may sing to you and not be silent. O LORD my God, I will give you thanks forever.

Psalm 34:3-4

Glorify the LORD with me; let us exalt his name together. I sought the LORD, and he answered me; he delivered me from all my fears.

Psalm 34:8

Taste and see that the LORD is good; blessed is the man who takes refuge in him.

Psalm 34:18

The LORD is close to the brokenhearted and saves those who are crushed in spirit.

Psalm 37:3-6

Trust in the LORD and do good; dwell in the land and enjoy safe pasture. Delight yourself in the LORD and he will give you the desires of your heart. Commit your way to the LORD; trust in him and he will do this: He will make your righteousness shine like the dawn, the justice of your cause like the noonday sun.

Psalm 40:2
He lifted me out of the slimy pit, out of the mud and mire; he set my feet on a rock and gave me a firm place to stand.

Psalm 46:1-3
God is our refuge and strength, an ever-present help in trouble. Therefore we will not fear, though the earth give way and the mountains fall into the heart of the sea, though its waters roar and foam and the mountains quake with their surging.

Psalm 46:10
Be still and know that I am God.

Psalm 51:10-12
Create in me a pure heart, O God, and renew a steadfast spirit within me. Do not cast me from your presence or take your Holy Spirit from me. Restore to me the joy of your salvation and grant me a willing spirit, to sustain me.

Psalm 84:11-12
For the LORD God is a sun and shield; the LORD bestows favor and

honor; no good thing does he withhold from those whose walk is blameless. O LORD Almighty, blessed is the man who trusts in you.

Proverbs 2:7-8
He holds victory in store for the upright, he is a shield to those whose walk is blameless, for he guards the course of the just and protects the way of his faithful ones.

Proverbs 3:5-6
Trust in the LORD with all your heart and lean not on your own understanding; in all your ways acknowledge him, and he will make your paths straight.

Isaiah 26:3
You will keep in perfect peace him whose mind is steadfast, because he trusts in you.

Isaiah 43:19
See, I am doing a new thing! Now it springs up; do you not perceive it? I am making a way in the desert and streams in the wasteland.

Jeremiah 29:11
"For I know the plans I have for you," declares the LORD, "plans to

prosper you and not to harm you, plans to give you hope and a future."

Jeremiah 33:3
Call to me and I will answer you and tell you great and unsearchable things you do not know.

John 1:12
Yet to all who received him, to those who believed in his name, he gave the right to become children of God.

Romans 4:3
Abraham believed God, and it was credited to him as righteousness.

Romans 4:20-21
Yet he [Abraham] did not waver through unbelief regarding the promise of God, but was strengthened in his faith and gave glory to God, being fully persuaded that God had power to do what he had promised.

Romans 5:8
But God demonstrates his own love for us in this: While we were still sinners, Christ died for us.

Romans 8:18

I consider that our present sufferings are not worth comparing with the glory that will be revealed in us.

Romans 8:24-25

For in this hope we were saved. But hope that is seen is no hope at all. Who hopes for what he already has? But if we hope for what we do not yet have, we wait for it patiently.

Romans 8:37-39

No, in all these things we are more than conquerors through him who loved us. For I am convinced that neither death nor life, neither angels nor demons, neither the present nor the future, nor any powers, neither height nor depth, nor anything else in all creation, will be able to separate us from the love of God that is in Christ Jesus our Lord.

1 Corinthians 2:9

However, as it is written: "No eye has seen, no ear has heard, no mind has conceived what God has prepared for those who love him."

2 Corinthians 3:18

And we, who with unveiled faces all reflect the Lord's glory, are being transformed into his likeness with ever-increasing glory, which comes from the Lord, who is the Spirit.

2 Corinthians 4:8-10

We are hard pressed on every side, but not crushed; perplexed, but not in despair; persecuted, but not abandoned; struck down, but not destroyed. We always carry around in our body the death of Jesus, so that the life of Jesus may also be revealed in our body.

2 Corinthians 4:18

So we fix our eyes not on what is seen, but on what is unseen. For what is seen is temporary, but what is unseen is eternal.

2 Corinthians 12:9

But he said to me, "My grace is sufficient for you, for my power is made perfect in weakness."

Ephesians 1:18-19

I pray also that the eyes of your heart may be enlightened in order that you may know the hope to which he has called you, the riches of his glorious inheritance in the saints, and his incomparably great power for us who believe.

Philippians 1:9-11

And this is my prayer: that your love may abound more and more in knowledge and depth of insight, so that you may be able to discern what is best and may be pure and blameless until the day of Christ, filled with the fruit of righteousness that comes through Jesus Christ—to the glory and praise of God.

Philippians 4:9

Whatever you have learned or received or heard from me, or seen in me—put it into practice. And the God of peace will be with you.

Philippians 4:11-13

I have learned to be content whatever the circumstances. I know what it is to be in need, and I know what it is to have plenty. I have learned the secret of being content in any and every situation, whether well fed or hungry, whether living in plenty or in want. I can do everything through him who gives me strength.

2 Timothy 1:7

For God did not give us a spirit of timidity, but a spirit of power, of love and of self-discipline.

2 Timothy 4:7-8

I have fought the good fight, I have finished the race, I have kept the faith. Now there is in store for me the crown of righteousness, which the Lord, the righteous Judge, will award to me on that day—and not only to me, but also to all who have longed for his appearing.

Hebrews 4:14-16

Therefore, since we have a great high priest who has gone through the heavens, Jesus the Son of God, let us hold firmly to the faith we profess. For we do not have a high priest who is unable to sympathize with our weaknesses, but we have one who has been tempted in every way, just as we are—yet was without sin. Let us then approach the throne of grace with confidence, so that we may receive mercy and find grace to help us in our time of need.

Hebrews 10:23

Let us hold unswervingly to the hope we profess, for he who promised is faithful.

Hebrews 10:35-37

So do not throw away your confidence; it will be richly rewarded. You need to persevere so that when you have done the will of God, you will receive what he has promised. For in just a very little while, "He who is coming will come and will not delay."

Hebrews 11:1
Now faith is being sure of what we hope for and certain of what we do not see.

Hebrews 13:15-16
Through Jesus, therefore, let us continually offer to God a sacrifice of praise—the fruit of lips that confess his name. And do not forget to do good and to share with others, for with such sacrifices God is pleased.

James 1:12
Blessed is the man who perseveres under trial, because when he has stood the test, he will receive the crown of life that God has promised to those who love him.

1 Peter 1:13
Therefore, prepare your minds for action; be self-controlled; set your hope fully on the grace to be given you when Jesus Christ is revealed.

1 Peter 4:12-13
Dear friends, do not be surprised at the painful trial you are suffering,

as though something strange were happening to you. But rejoice that you participate in the sufferings of Christ, so that you may be overjoyed when his glory is revealed.

1 Peter 5:7
Cast all your anxiety on him because he cares for you.

Revelation 21:1-5
Then I saw a new heaven and a new earth, for the first heaven and the first earth had passed away, and there was no longer any sea. I saw the Holy City, the new Jerusalem, coming down out of heaven from God, prepared as a bride beautifully dressed for her husband. And I heard a loud voice from the throne saying, "Now the dwelling of God is with men, and he will live with them. They will be his people, and God himself will be with them and be their God. He will wipe every tear from their eyes. There will be no more death or mourning or crying or pain, for the old order of things has passed away." He who was seated on the throne said, "I am making everything new!"

Deborah Dortzbach & W. Meredith Long

THE AIDS CRISIS

What We Can Do

IVP Books

An imprint of InterVarsity Press
Downers Grove, Illinois

InterVarsity Press
P.O. Box 1400, Downers Grove, IL 60515-1426
World Wide Web: www.ivpress.com
E-mail: mail@ivpress.com

InterVarsity Press® is the book-publishing division of InterVarsity Christian Fellowship/USA®, a student movement
active on campus at hundreds of universities, colleges and schools of nursing in the United States of America, and a
member movement of the International Fellowship of Evangelical Students. For information about local and regional
activities, write Public Relations Dept., InterVarsity Christian Fellowship/USA, 6400 Schroeder Rd., P.O. Box 7895,
Madison, WI 53707-7895, or visit the IVCF website at <www.intervarsity.org>.

The life stories told in this book are true, though in some cases the names have been changed.

Interior photos are used by permission of World Relief.

Design: Cindy Kiple
Images: Per-Anders Petterson/Getty Images

ISBN-10: 0-8308-3372-2
ISBN-13: 978-0-8308-3372-6

Printed in the United States of America ∞

Library of Congress Cataloging-in-Publication Data

Dortzbach, Deborah.
    The AIDs crisis: what we can do / Deborah Dortzbach and Meredith
    Long.
        p. cm.
    Includes bibliographical references.
    ISBN-13: 978-0-8308-3372-6 (pbk.: alk. paper)
    ISBN-10: 0-8308-3372-2 (pbk.: alk. paper)
    1. AIDS (Disease)—Religious aspects—Christianity. 2. Church work
with the sick. I. Long, W. Meredith. II. Title.
    BV4460.7.D67 2006
    261.8'321969792—dc22
                                                                        2006030073

| P | 19 | 18 | 17 | 16 | 15 | 14 | 13 | 12 | 11 | 10 | 9 | 8 | 7 | 6 | 5 | 4 | 3 | 2 | 1 |
| Y | 21 | 20 | 19 | 18 | 17 | 16 | 15 | 14 | 13 | 12 | 11 | 10 | 09 | 08 | 07 | 06 | | | | |

Contents

Dedication and Acknowledgments

We dedicate this book to Sukunthea, who you will meet in chapter one, and to the tens of thousands of those like her who, in the name of Christ, help individuals, families and communities bear the burden of AIDS. These men, women, youth and children, who are often known only to their families and communities, are the feet, arms, hands and heart of Christ. They are our heroes and teachers, and truly great in the kingdom of God.

We deeply thank World Relief's HIV/AIDS team who helped us craft this book on top of all of their other work. Joanna Mayhew and Piper Purcell researched, compiled and helped to assemble the book. Piper wrote the discussion questions, grounding the book in ways that we would not have thought of. Dr. Lisa Firth skillfully but gently coached us in transforming what we first wrote into what we really wanted to say.

Dr. Deborah T. Hung of Brigham and Women's Hospital and the Harvard Medical School somehow found time to critically review the medical and scientific information in the book, helping us to simplify and accurately express the great complexity of HIV infection and treatment. Any mistakes and omissions are ours and certainly not hers.

We are honored that InterVarsity Press asked us to write about what has been a central part of our lives for so long. Our senior editor, Cindy Bunch, along with Lisa Rieck and many other readers and copyeditors targeted our writing and vastly improved it.

Finally, we thank World Relief for supporting us in the time-consuming task of writing but even more for fielding effective AIDS-related ministries. All of the royalties from the sales of the book will be reinvested in World Relief's global ministries, mobilizing and empowering God's church in the world to minister in Christ's name to their communities and nations.

Introduction

WHY WE WROTE THIS BOOK

By the mid-1980s we—the global community—knew what the HIV virus does and the ways it spreads from one person to another. Public health experts knew in what parts of the world and in which communities it had become resident. There was hope that an AIDS vaccine or a cure would be found, but at the time there was no effective treatment for the disease. With those facts established, medical science didn't need the gift of prophecy to predict a bleak future concerning AIDS. Barring a medical miracle, millions were going to die.

Since then, AIDS has shaped our personal and professional ministries. This book reflects the lessons we've learned from over twenty years of leading teams of people from many nations giving hands, feet and voice to compassion in the face of AIDS. Hundreds of thousands of people affected by AIDS have been touched by Christ's love by thousands of church volunteers who visit, help, teach and counsel in their own communities. The programs developed through churches to prevent AIDS and care for families affected by AIDS have been recognized for their professional excellence as well as the compassion that animates them.

As Christians, none of us can confront AIDS without also confronting core issues that define us. We confront our own attitudes and actions regarding sex, sexual behaviors and people who are diagnosed with AIDS. We confront the structural evils that mold the environment in which HIV flourishes. We confront the conflicts between grace and judgment that influence our cultures as well as our own character. We confront the role and power of the church in the world. We who are Westerners eventually confront our deeply held cultural belief that solving any global problem is just a question of will, strategy and resources.

We've written this book first of all to provoke these confrontations as we describe AIDS in the context of life and hands-on interventions. Our reflections are woven into the fabric of the text. We have been deeply changed by AIDS and the issues surrounding it—changes that not only define what we do, but make us who we are.

The church no longer has any choice about whether to respond; we can only decide *how* we will respond. Even though God will not call most of you reading this book into specific AIDS-related ministries, you will nonetheless be shaped by honestly confronting AIDS. As you read, we invite you to encounter God and yourself.

We've also written this book for Christians and churches who are exposed to the reality of AIDS firsthand or who may wish to be involved through ministry. As a result of reading this book, we hope that you will examine your expectations and attitudes about AIDS-related ministry. As you encounter the enormity of the AIDS disaster, we hope you will be humbled in the face of this disease and that this will constantly drive you back to God for power and wisdom, and to others for help and discernment. We hope that you will determine not to go it alone in ministry but to work hand in hand with many others—even with people with whom you may disagree— in confronting issues of sexuality, HIV and AIDS.

We hope that this book will inform the ministry approaches and strategies of the ever-increasing number of churches and agencies that are engaging in AIDS-related activities.

Finally, we hope that those who read this book will commit to excellence in ministry—a recognition that doing good demands not only passion and power but also discipline and learning.

Three additional features of this book will help you in your personal and corporate response to AIDS. First, at the end of each chapter, personal reflection and action questions will help you define your response to AIDS. The reflection questions guide you in how you will apply the content of the chapter to yourself, and the action questions guide you in how you will respond toward others. A study guide at the end of the book, designed primarily for group discussion, will help you integrate the content of the book into a more comprehensive approach. Finally, an extensive list of resources, also at the end of the book, will help support your continued reflections, further study and response.

As the apostle John approached the end of his ministry, he wrote to those who had become precious to him. "Dear children, let us not love with words or tongue but with actions and in truth" (1 John 3:18). This is our prayer for those who encounter AIDS and Christ through this book.

Deb Dortzbach
Meredith Long

ONE

Understanding the AIDS Problem

I (Deb) will never forget the first time I shook hands with a man with AIDS. It was in my own country in the basement of a cold, stone church. His face was a mottled purple with cracked and swollen lips. His hands and arms were riddled with marks and scabs like I remembered chicken pox looking on my brothers and sisters. I could hear my mother saying when my sister lay limp with fever, "Don't get too close. You might get it."

Everything in me stepped back. I was repulsed. What if I get it? What if I give it? Perhaps this volunteer work is going a bit too far. It's one thing to expose myself, but what about exposing my husband and my children?

I wasn't asleep to helping people in need. I had chosen a nursing career to guide me toward others, not away from them. But there was a kind of indifference in me I didn't know I had—a self-protection that meant I recoiled when pushed to the edge of suffering myself. I was willing to see suffering and maybe to help alleviate it. I wasn't willing to suffer myself. I didn't realize then that helping those who suffer from AIDS would invite a vulnerability that would shape my own struggle to suffer with them—not in getting the disease but in becoming so affected by AIDS that it would change my life.

It shocked me to consider how conditional my concern for others was. I was a pastor's daughter; throughout my childhood my father brought home drunken men to dry out and homeless families who wandered into the church. My lifelong journey with my physically and mentally handicapped twin brother taught me how to care for the defenseless. I was prepared for the world even though I lived sheltered from it.

The purple-faced man gentled me with a smile, exposing a thick tongue and rims of frothy white sores on his lips and gums. His dark eyes glistened.

"Thanks for coming," he said, as a hint of strength pressed through his fingers to my hand cradling his.

I thought I knew how to give. This man taught me how to receive. He gave me the opportunity to understand more of his suffering—to explore deeper lessons of suffering and receive lessons about my own frailty, ambivalence, conditional love and sometimes impatient faith.

That was seventeen years ago. I've come to realize AIDS—not the people with AIDS—is still mysterious. In 1988 it looked confined, almost manageable. Most public health professionals thought changed behaviors within the homosexual community would turn things around. We believed we could apply the best of medical science, technology and epidemiology to a shrinking world and control it.

In the early years of the epidemic, the international AIDS conference convened every year to share and debate the most recent advances in the molecular configurations and DNA of the virus that causes AIDS, convincing us that keys to unlocking a cure were within reach. The virus seemed contained within the homosexual community and pockets of cities with offbeat bars and alleys.

Most people felt immune. "If we don't get close, we won't catch it," we told ourselves.

Christians didn't bother to get involved. In North America we thought it was a gay disease—a justifiable gay disease, in fact, that showed the consequences of sexual sin. So the bands played on. Our worlds never intersected, and we liked that. We wouldn't catch it that way.

We couldn't have been more wrong. AIDS isn't confined and never really was. It's just hidden much of the time. The virus copies itself, disguises itself and, with new configurations of viral parts, strengthens itself to do the sinister work of destroying the very system the body uses to defend itself from such invasions. The body withers, defeated by a particle sixty times smaller than a red blood cell.

AIDS is a disease that brings death to people in the most productive stage of life—teens and adults between fifteen and fifty. Most people get it by having sex with someone whom they don't know is infected. The tiny virus—passed through sexual fluids, fresh blood and sometimes breast milk—cycles from aggressive attacks and periods of rapid multiplication to sinister games of hide-and-seek within the body. Its effects may tarry, but it will never leave. Usually affected people have no idea that they've been attacked or that they have the potential to infect others. Years later, the virus surfaces with vile vengeance and oscillating destruction. Short periods of fever, cough and diarrhea give way to months and years of illness. Common infections, including tuberculosis (TB), fail to yield to treatment, becoming death traps, joined by cancers, neurological problems and sometimes blindness and deafness.

AIDS is most often caused by sex, bringing one of the most troubling paradoxes of the disease. How is it that the most intimate act designed by God to be enjoyed by two married individuals has become the conduit of death for many millions? How can the pinnacle of pleasure become the promoter of pain?

Some questions are best not answered. Not because there aren't answers, but because answers are incomplete. As soon as we are categorical about AIDS resulting from adultery, we learn the risk of infection is greatest in Africa among women who have done nothing but be faithful to their husbands. As soon as we hide from homosexuality issues, we learn that the struggle for sexual purity is deep within our own soul, and our own pointing fingers forbid an honest look. As soon as we are unforgiving toward those involved in sex before marriage, we discover hidden Internet accounts of pornography among those we deeply trust.

The Story of Chrub

Lim's thick, dark hair and petite frame were moneymakers, and she used them well. She made a living selling her body.

Every night before making her way to the low end of town near the river, Lim made food for her daughter, Chrub, then got herself ready for work, adorning her dark eyes with precise streaks of black liner. After splashing herself with perfume, she left the

house. Her silken hair flowed freely behind her as she took the motorcycle taxi to her
business on the other side of Phnom Penh, Cambodia.

Men came all night long, some of them bringing boys—twelve, thirteen, fourteen
years old. Lim was paid to introduce boys to sex. They were to practice and have fun
with her so they could be experienced and restrained with their wives when it was time
to get married. It is a kind of initiation, widely practiced and accepted, though not
talked about except among the boys themselves.

As Chrub grew older, Lim prepared her daughter to learn the job, introducing her
to clients. A young, beautiful virgin would produce a fat income.

There was little choice for Chrub. She soon became part of the routine, sleeping
during the day and working at night. She hated her job, and she hated herself. In fact,
she wondered if anyone loved her. She felt trapped. With little education, no available
jobs, and surrounded by others who were selling sex, she had little choice. Many girls
and women in her business did not have a choice.

She never used a condom.

Only one person in her family understood her—her grandmother, Sivon. Chrub
often fled to her during the day, just to talk and be who she really was—a person, not
a body. Her grandmother talked about her own childhood and the dreams she had for
Chrub to have a different life.

Less than ten years after the killing-field era of the Khmer Rouge that
Sivon had lived through, a new era of death began. Fueled by the sexual ex-
ploits of the military, commercial sex workers and injecting drug users, the
killing fields shifted from the countryside to the bedrooms, street corners
and heroin hideouts—this time through a virus. "AIDS is even more serious
than war," Cambodian Prime Minister Hun Sen warned in 1999. "In some
cases whole families have been wiped out—the father is dead, the mother is
dead and later the children die of AIDS too."[1]

Throughout this book, we are going to be introducing you to real people who have
AIDS. In particular you will learn more of Chrub's story. She was found by a church

in Cambodia who scoured neighborhoods looking for people living with AIDS, many of whom were rejected by their family members.

Chrub, a young, strong, beautiful woman, had a horrible sickness. It had started like any other illness. She had improved after a couple of days. Life had proceeded as usual. In fact, years had passed. Sickness had come and gone but now came more frequently. As coughing and fevers, diarrhea and weight loss set in, treatment failed to bring lasting results. Chrub grew weaker. There were days she could not manage to climb the few wooden-plank stairs to her platform living space tucked above the marshy muck of Phnom Penh's streets. She no longer went to work or carried water. She lay limp and pencil thin, her striking dark eyes piercing sleepless nights.

People began to talk. There was only one explanation for a sickness that doesn't go away no matter what you do, especially when it comes to someone so young, they thought. Few spoke about it, but everyone stayed away.

Sukunthea, a member of the Way of Hope Church in Phnom Penh, completed a workshop on basic care for people living with AIDS, and she set out to put her knowledge into practice. She discovered Chrub, abandoned in her home with only Sivon to watch over her.

In her classes, Sukunthea had learned how to approach homes with politeness and respect. She explained who she was and why she had come—to help people in the neighborhood too sick to help themselves—to Chrub and Sivon. "What might I do for you?" she asked.

She began with simple tasks—fetching water, making rice gruel, washing diarrhea-soaked clothes. Day after day she came, and day after day Chrub grew weaker.

The neighbors kept talking, but from a distance. Doesn't the visitor know that home is cursed? Why does she come? And why isn't she getting sick, too?

WHAT IS AIDS AND HOW DOES IT SPREAD?

Sukunthea's hope in the face of AIDS rested in her faith and her lack of fear. Sukunthea did not fear transmission from Chrub, because she knew and believed the facts about the disease. Many in Cambodia believe AIDS is a curse. To go near it is to fall under it. Because it is so feared, signs are sometimes posted near the door—not an AIDS red ribbon pledging support, nor a red cross symbolizing help, but a skull and crossbones warning of evil and death.

Unlike Chrub's neighbors, Sukunthea knew that AIDS is not spread through airborne transmission such as coughing or sneezing. It's not passed through handshakes, food preparation or consumption—even when sharing the same bowl or chopsticks.

What does transmit HIV is the mixing of sexual fluids through sexual intercourse—vaginal, anal and sometimes oral—where one member's body harbors the human immunodeficiency virus, HIV. This crafty virus invades and kills white blood cells that our bodies need to fight infections (including HIV). We are still discovering the mechanisms of how it operates. It attaches itself to receptor molecules on the outside of the white cell and fuses its own viral membrane with the cell's membrane. Then, through a series of extremely complicated and well-studied gyrations, it incorporates itself into the cell's blueprint, eventually resulting in the host cell's death. We still do not know exactly how it destroys.

Once inside the cell, the virus' blueprint becomes integrated into the cell's blueprint through a process known as reverse transcription. The virus becomes part and parcel of the host cell's nucleus. There it replicates, creating more viruses, as well as disabling the host.

The virus has a profound ability to survive inside the body, and so far nothing stops it. We cannot kill every single virus hiding inside an HIV-infected person, and so there is no cure yet. However, scientists have made enormous strides in limiting the replication of the invader. Antiretroviral medicines (ARVs), especially when used in combination, suppress the growth of HIV, most often preserving a person's immune system for a prolonged period of time, and resulting in many years of extended life. (A more detailed discussion of ARV treatment is in chapter eight.)

After a twenty-five page description of HIV and the process it goes through to destroy the body, Dr. Stephen Goff, researcher for the Department of Biochemistry and Molecular Biophysics at Columbia University, claims that the AIDS epidemic will go down in history as one of the greatest pandemics of all time. He concludes that because the virus "has evolved an efficient life cycle and a profoundly insidious lifestyle, it is likely that HIV will continue to be the cause of enormous human suffering throughout the world for many years to come."[2]

HIV is unstable outside the body where it is quickly destroyed by heat, drying and detergents. Though HIV may be detected in any body fluid including tears, sweat, saliva and urine, it needs white blood cells found in sufficient amounts in fresh blood, sexual fluids and breast milk to be transmitted to others.

This means it is hard to get HIV from others except through sex or fresh blood-to-blood contact. The virus may also be passed from an HIV-positive mother to her infant while pregnant, at birth, or after birth through breast-feeding.

The HIV virus is not easy to transmit, but the nature of the epidemic assures its spread. Up to ten years can pass between the time of infection and the onset of clinically recognizable AIDS. During that entire period, infected people can spread the virus to others and not even know they have it themselves.

As the authors of this book, we share our collective reflections and experiences over twenty years of wrestling with this virus, the trail of destruction left in its wake and the challenges in directing behavior to avoid new infections. We tell the stories of men, women and children affected not only by illnesses related to AIDS but also by the compounded sufferings of deeper poverty, broken relationships and abandonment. Some faces never leave our minds, nor do the sacrificial acts of kindness and dedication by caregivers, trainers, researchers and church members.

Our purpose is to press you not only to understand more as a concerned global citizen, but also to act—to examine your own life, attitudes and behaviors; to renew your lifelong covenants in your own families; to reach out to those in your community who wrestle with life itself as they live with AIDS; to become involved globally with prevention and care efforts; and to join many others in prayers for the alleviation of suffering and for a cure.

The impact of AIDS may frighten you or even overwhelm you. But what will stick with you long after you finish reading this book are the many examples of grace. Discover them. Reflect on them. Imitate them. And seek out God, the one who will always make sure there is enough grace to keep going.

TAKING THE NEXT STEPS

Personal Reflection

Imagine that you discover through a routine physical that you are HIV positive.

1. Who would you tell about your infection? Who would you choose not to tell? What does that tell you about the nature of this disease and of your relationships with those people?

2. Make a list of the questions that you would want to ask—to God, family members, friends, clinicians and others who have HIV.

Action Steps

1. If you know people who are HIV positive well enough, gently open the door in private conversation for them to tell their stories.

2. If you do not know anyone who is HIV positive, read some firsthand accounts or blogs written by people who are infected. What similarities and differences do you find in their stories? What seems to have made a difference in how well they have coped with the disease?

3. Pray for the thousands of men, women and children who will discover today that they are HIV positive.

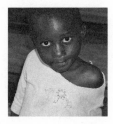

AIDS Around the World

Elizabeth is eleven years old and lives in Kenya with her mother and two brothers. Her father died of AIDS two years ago; her mother also has AIDS. When her father died, her uncles came and took all the family property, ejecting Elizabeth's family from their home and their only source of livelihood. Elizabeth had to stop going to school for two reasons: She had no money, and she had to care for her mother, who was becoming increasingly ill, and her two younger brothers.

When Elizabeth told her story to a church volunteer, she ended by saying, "If my father were alive, I would be the happiest girl in the whole world."

Elizabeth's struggles are far from over. She will probably face the death of her mother when she is twelve years old, and she will shoulder the entire responsibility for her younger siblings. She's confused about what to tell people who scorn AIDS as a generational curse and grapples daily with the stigma and rejection, even from family members. There will be no family income and no way to get it unless she begins giving sexual favors to "sugar daddies" who prey on girls in her neighborhood. If she ever gets back to school, there will be a shortage of teachers because they too are dying of AIDS. Since her mother's illness, the fields lie fallow. There is no food in the grain bin.

Elizabeth's story highlights the impact of the AIDS crisis on families, communities and the future. Even if we were able to intercept the fourteen thousand new infections that happen each day and eventually declare our world AIDS free, the legacy of twenty-five years of colossal devastation to individuals—particularly children—to families and to our communities will hound us for generations to come.

THE HISTORY OF AIDS

Since 1982 when AIDS was first observed in New York and San Francisco among homosexual men, the HIV virus has escaped boundaries designed to constrain it. Current HIV infection among gay men is completely overshadowed by the sheer numbers of the global epidemic. Our borderless world has become an open playground for infection. Today not one country in the world escapes the ravage. As medical anthropologist Susan Hunter has observed, "HIV/AIDS is fast becoming the worst human disaster the world has ever known. Even if a cure is found tomorrow, the toll of death and suffering by 2010 will far exceed any other recorded human catastrophe, any other previous epidemic, natural disaster, war, or incident of genocidal violence."[1]

The infection spread quietly, wildly. In the early years, countries of global wealth and influence were affected: the United States, France, Spain and Brazil. Scientists, intrigued by the elusive nature of the disease, raced to identify the offending pathogen and ended up arguing over who reached the conclusion first—Robert Gallo from America or Luc Montagnier of France. Discovering the HIV virus was just the beginning. Remarkable progress was made early on. Pharmaceutical companies rushed to secure patents for anti-AIDS drugs. As the epidemic gained momentum, confident researchers plunged into the search for a cure.

The International AIDS Conference began, eventually bringing together the largest number of people ever to study a single disease. Global scientists, health practitioners, political leaders, drug companies, policymakers and community workers now meet biannually to put the best of practice and research into the petri dish for closer examination and decision making.

The vectors of infection were quickly isolated. Those at highest risk were men who had sex with men, people who shared needles to shoot drugs, and commercial sex workers and their clients. From these high-risk groups the infection radiated outward into the community. The first line of defense against AIDS in many countries was to target high-risk groups with strong messages of condom use and clean needles to prevent the spread of infection into the general population.

Soon, seemingly healthy men and women in Africa began to show the same symptoms as gay men in the United States—lumpy necks, incessant diarrhea and thinning bodies—but at a greatly accelerated pace. Twenty- and thirty-year-old men died in battle or in accidents, but not often from sickness. Heads turned. Desperately ill men and women searched the African countryside for traditional medicines and healing. One entrepreneur in Kenya hawked "the chameleon medicine," comprised of colored earth to dye white blood cells red or orange or green since AIDS attacks only white blood cells. Africans knew how to survive drought, famine, war, disease, greedy leaders and plunging economies or no economy at all. AIDS was just another trouble to face. A way would be found. The hunt was on.

But neither modern science nor traditional medicines were able to break the power of AIDS. No way was found. HIV spread rapidly in a global environment that long had been prepared to nurture its growth. In the global South, poverty separated men seeking work from their wives and the constraints of rural communities. The men found sexual relief in the arms of women who themselves were driven by poverty into the sex trade.

In Uganda, researchers discovered the now-famous alleyways of transmission. Major transport routes traced a flaming corridor of AIDS across the country. Truckers bringing goods overland from the Indian Ocean ignited an AIDS pathway fueled by their truck-stop girlfriends. Back home, waiting wives and their newborns grew sick and died. A half century of community health advancement in reducing mortality of children under five years, protecting women in childbirth, and controlling malnutrition and infectious diseases was halted and, in many places, reversed.

Many countries began to reap an ever-increasing harvest of death from chronically inadequate investments in their health systems now overwhelmed by AIDS-related diseases. Even before the time of antiretroviral therapies, the costs of HIV testing, the screening of blood donations and the treatment of opportunistic infections were far too great for these most-affected countries to absorb. Africa has borne the greatest burden of this disease.

HIV/AIDS TIMELINE

(Summarized from the Kaiser Family Foundation: The Global HIV/AIDS Epidemic: A Timeline of Key Milestones, <www.kff.org>.)

1981

The time of HIV/AIDS officially begins as the CDC reports the outbreak of rare pneumonia and other illnesses among gay men in San Francisco.

1982

The CDC names the disease—AIDS or Acquired Immune Deficiency Syndrome. Haitians, injecting drug users and hemophiliacs join gay men on the list of people most at risk.

1983

The Public Health Service in the United States publishes the first guidelines to prevention of infection through sexual contact and blood transfusions.

1984

Luc Montagnier and Robert Gallo isolate the virus, later named HIV.

1985

As each region of the world reports at least one case of AIDS, the first International Conference on HIV/AIDS is held in Atlanta. The first lab test for HIV antibodies is licensed. The first guidelines for the prevention of mother-to-child transmission are published.

1986

President Reagan talks about AIDS in public for the first time. Surgeon General C. Everett Koop promotes the use of condoms for prevention and ignites an ongoing debate among evangelicals.

1987

The first antiretroviral drug is approved. WHO begins its Global Program on AIDS. The AIDS Service Organization emerges as an effective indigenous agency responding to AIDS in Uganda, the first country to capture global attention to the developing AIDS crisis in Africa. The AIDS quilt, the publication of And the Band Played On by Randy Shilts, and the creation of ACT UP (AIDS Coalition to Unleash Power) focus public attention on AIDS and the politics of AIDS. The first conference is held in the U.S. on AIDS and people of color.

1988

World AIDS Day is observed for the first time. It is first reported that HIV-infected women in Africa outnumber the HIV-infected men. Pressure for the rapid approval of new antiretroviral medicines increases.

1989

AIDS activists accelerate the frequency and intensity of protests regarding access to ARV medicines. People who are living with AIDS are given access to ARVs still in clinical trials.

1990

Protests lead to a boycott of the 6th International AIDS Conference in San Francisco. Ryan White dies and the Ryan White Act provides public funding for community-based care and treatment of AIDS.

1991

The red ribbon becomes the global symbol for AIDS awareness.

HIV/AIDS TIMELINE (CONTINUED)

1992
The first rapid HIV test is licensed.

1994
AZT therapy is first identified and recommended as a method to radically reduce mother-to-child transmission.

1995
HAART (highly active antiretroviral therapy) begins with the introduction of the first protease inhibitor. The first White House Conference on AIDS is held.

1996-1997
UNAIDS begins operation. Brazil is the first nation to begin nationwide distribution of ARV therapy. AIDS-related deaths in the U.S. decrease by 40% because of HAART.

1998-1999
The Congressional Black Caucus and African American leaders in the United States proclaim a "state of emergency" within their community, and the Minority AIDS Initiative begins. The downside of HAART, growing resistance and side effects, begins to become apparent. Grassroots lobbying for access to ARVs in Africa begins to gear up. The growing threat of AIDS to the Russian Federation, Ukraine and Central Asia gains new visibility.

2000
The International AIDS Conference is first held in Africa, in Durban. UNAIDS and WHO begin to orchestrate growing pressure on pharmaceutical companies to lower the cost of their medicines and make them increasingly available in Africa and other impoverished areas. The reduction of TB, AIDS and malaria is included as one of the Millennium Development Goals.

2001
Twenty years after the first case of AIDS was reported, the United Nations General Assembly convenes its first global meeting on AIDS.

2002
The Global Fund to Fight AIDS, TB and Malaria approves its first round of grants. HIV infection becomes the greatest global killer of men and women 15-59 years old. The publication of *AIDS in China, New Millennium—Titanic Challenge* by UNAIDS focuses global attention on the growing threat that AIDS poses to China and India, the two most populous countries in the world.

2003
The President's Emergency Plan for AIDS Relief (PEPFAR) is initiated by the United States. The WHO announces the "3 x 5 initiative" to place three million people from the developing world on ARV treatment by 2005. The William J. Clinton Foundation negotiates significant price reductions on HIV/AIDS drugs for the developing world.

2004-2006
The AIDS cocktail is first reduced to a single-dose pill combining medicines from different pharmaceutical companies. By the end of 2004, 700,000 people in the developing world have started ARV therapy. The UN General Assembly convenes a high-level meeting to track progress against the goals set in 2001. India overtakes South Africa as the country reporting the greatest number of people living with HIV or AIDS.

In well-resourced countries the debate concerning AIDS fractured along the same cultural and political fault lines as gay awareness and rights. The political action of gay groups, who were most threatened by the disease, mobilized awareness and an accelerated response. Over time in the United States, as the pattern of HIV infection and the burden of AIDS began to shift from gay men, who possessed a strong political voice, to injecting (IDU) drug users among people of color, who had little political influence and few advocates, awareness of AIDS in the United States also faded and the aggressiveness of the prevention response slowed.

AIDS acquired its stigma, nurtured by poverty and fueled by death, fear, unchallenged ignorance about its transmission and prevention, and its association with sinful behaviors and oft-condemned people groups. The stigma nourished cultures of denial, silence and inaction everywhere. In the most severely affected and vulnerable regions, the consequences were grave. Optimism almost vanished from international meetings.

AIDS TODAY

The total number of people living with HIV is nearly forty million and rising, double the number ten years ago. In 2005, 2.8 million people died of AIDS; half a million of them were children under fifteen. Nearly eight thousand people die each day as a result of the AIDS epidemic. Over thirteen hundred of them are children. By 2010, 25 million children will have been orphaned by AIDS.

And all this is in spite of the fact that in the past twenty-five years more resources of time, money, skill and brainpower have been spent on AIDS than on any other illness in history. In that short time, HIV has spread to every country in the world, infecting 65 million people and killing 25 million. And the impact of AIDS on the global population has not yet reached its peak. By 2015, the total population of the sixty countries most affected by AIDS is estimated to be 115 million less than it would be in the absence of AIDS.[2]

AIDS IN AFRICA

The bad news for many in Africa was that AIDS looked like a curse. Many believed that if you found a counter curse—something more powerful—the curse would be broken. Reality set in. The curse-breaker was not a medicine or charm. Rather, men and women either spread or prevented the spread of HIV through their own sexual behavior.

The world joined the fight. The United Nations launched a new initiative, UNAIDS, and commissioned the integration of all the UN bodies, making UNAIDS the one hub that marshaled resources from all agencies. Countries established AIDS commissions, initially under ministries of health and then often reporting directly to the country's leader.

No class, country, race, gender or religion was spared from AIDS. Only the elderly who had stopped having sex and children aged six to fourteen normally escaped infection. Children of those ages were too old to have caught it from infected mothers, and most had not yet become sexually active.

Infection rates in eastern Africa soared during the 1990s. In some villages in Tanzania, Uganda and Kenya only the extremely old and the young children remained.

South Africa had been distracted by its battle against another evil. In 1994 apartheid ended, and blacks and whites celebrated the election of Nelson Mandela as president. Euphoria turned to agony as the casualties of the hidden but incredibly deadly battle against AIDS became apparent at the turn of this century. HIV infection had never practiced apartheid, so the liberated peoples were dying. South Africa engaged in the battle reluctantly and far too late.

Other countries fought different battles and lost. Rwanda lost one out of eight citizens to genocide and the war that followed. Armies and rebels in Mozambique, Angola, Sierra Leone, Burundi, Liberia, Congo, Côte d'Ivoire, Zimbabwe, Chad, Sudan, Eritrea and Ethiopia fought for supremacy. New ideologies and alliances, leaders, and even a new country emerged. Economic battles forced men to pack for the cities in search of work as they pursued an elusive vision to educate their children and to replace mud, grass and wooden structures with more permanent homes for their families. All too many returned home to die along with the wives they infected. The veneer of peace and economic development eroded with the deaths of these hopeful young people, the first generation to grow up in postcolonial freedom.

The future is grim for many African youth. Nine in ten children (under fifteen years old) who are infected with HIV live in sub-Saharan Africa.[3] Today, young people born in South Africa, Botswana, Swaziland, Namibia, Mozambique, Zambia and Lesotho have only a one in two chance of ever reaching their life goals. The rest will die of AIDS first. Women are particularly vulnerable. In some countries in Africa, three-fourths of all young people infected with the virus are women.[4] In general, African women are three times more likely to be infected than their male counterparts.

Famines, the ancient killers in Africa, are now caused not only by drought and war but also because there are not enough healthy farmers to tend the fields.

Africa has only 10 percent of the world's population but bears almost 64 percent of the global burden of AIDS. This cruel reality is heaped on top of other deeply troubling problems of growing poverty and ethnic conflict. Country after country reports escalating AIDS rates with the southern region leading the continent. Swaziland, Botswana, Namibia, South Africa and Lesotho report that approximately 30 percent of their pregnant women are HIV positive. In Swaziland, 43 percent of all pregnant women attending prenatal clinics carry HIV along with their child, more than a tenfold increase over the 4 percent of twelve years ago.[5]

Slowly, however, we are beginning to make a difference. The percentage of adults infected with HIV (prevalence) has declined in Kenya, Zimbabwe and the urban areas of Burkina Faso. In each of these countries, young people have chosen to delay their first sexual experience, to have fewer partners once they begin sexual activity, and to increasingly use condoms.

Fidele from Rwanda described life after his AIDS diagnosis to First Lady Laura Bush when she visited a church on a tour of programs funded through the President's Emergency Plan for AIDS Relief.

My name is Nsengiyumva Fidele. I am forty-eight years old, and I have five children. I learned I was HIV positive in July of 2002. I was full of fear and sorrow. After two weeks I made the decision to start an HIV/AIDS program in my church to help those who are not HIV positive to protect themselves, and to help those who are positive to deal with it well. I went to the leaders of the Friends Church. They told me that they had been praying about this for some time, but they didn't have anyone who could start this ministry. The church leaders and I saw that this was now the Lord's will.

This plan started well in August of 2002. That's when we started an association of HIV-positive people called The Good Samaritan. In October of that year I went to a training of trainers at World Relief. When I left there I had the burden to tell my story to others. But this was not possible because my wife still hadn't felt that same burden. She began to feel that burden later but she passed away in March of 2003 before we could start this ministry together.

After going to the second training, I found that I could do nothing but tell my story to others in my church. I wanted my story to help stop the stigma and shame that was common in many churches. I also wanted people to protect themselves from AIDS. I continued sharing my story openly in many other places in the country, and now we have many different associations for people living with AIDS.

The purpose I now have is to help church leaders who are HIV positive to be open about it, because they are good vehicles of hope among the community. I now have hope. I weighed 57 kilograms (125 lb.) when I started these programs, and now I weigh 71 kilograms (156 lb.). I haven't even started on antiretrovirals yet. So I still believe that I have a long time to fight the AIDS virus, to give my testimony, and to give advice to those around me.

For me, living with AIDS is the path through which God has chosen to use me. It's true, in my blood there is the AIDS virus, but there is also the blood of Jesus. I trust and do not doubt that Jesus' blood in me has more power than that of the AIDS virus. So I am not defeated by this virus. I stand firmly on God's word from Psalms 118:17, "I will not die but live [eternally], and proclaim what the Lord has done."[6]

AIDS IN ASIA

Chen stepped forward during a workshop break for church members in China's Hengyang City. Pulling the sleeve of his sweater up past his elbow, he asked me (Deb), "Do you think I can get AIDS by touching someone with it? I'm taking care of a drug addict who has AIDS."

A quick glance at his forearms revealed telltale tracks of drug use—scars and veins stripped. "Tell me your story," I asked. "Have you gone to take an HIV test yourself?"

His story mesmerized me, not so much because of the depths of pain and rejection he experienced, but because of the way he took his pain and transformed it into service. Among his former buddies, he was the only one strong enough to help care for the others. He had ten other friends who had AIDS.

After the break, Chen challenged the group as he recounted his own experience.

> I thank God that he sent me here because for more than ten years I was doing drugs, but Jesus gave me his love. In the last two days [of training], I can see that Jesus' love is here. We need to wake up, use our eyes to see the reality around us. If you get out to see someone with AIDS every month, that is a great plan. I have been living with a man with AIDS. I stay and help him twenty-four hours a day.
>
> Frankly speaking, after ten years, China's problem in AIDS will be very serious. The church is a very good organization to let people with AIDS know that we love them. We can kneel and pray with them. Many brothers pray for me. It is God who gives this love to others with AIDS.

Did you know people with AIDS are very depressed? Did you know if you are an AIDS patient not even a policeman will touch you because they are afraid? We have an opportunity to save the AIDS patient's body, save the AIDS patient's spirit, and prevent them from being seen as a criminal but instead as a person. I know so much now [because of God's help and the church] but [those infected] lack the good news of God's love.

What Africa is today, Asia will be tomorrow—except much worse. The vast numbers of people in the region make the present trends in HIV infections deeply alarming. But Asia is a sleeping dragon. Asia has had opportunity to take warning but until recently chose instead to bury concern.

The sheer numbers of people at risk of HIV infection in Asia should have been reason enough to pursue prevention early on. Yet the two nations with the largest populations in the world, India and China, initially ignored warnings to take action. In most Asian countries little has been done to prepare for this disaster-in-the-making, with the notable exception of Thailand.

Aware that the economy rested on the enormous sex trade, Thailand took aggressive steps to break the foothold the virus was making. Political leaders openly admitted the problem, and top government organizations mobilized to execute a comprehensive and coordinated plan to achieve 100 percent condom use within the sex trade and military. The campaign made millions of condoms available, taught people about proper use, and required that every commercial sex worker use them with clients. The campaign was hailed as a huge success for aborting a wide-scale, generalized epidemic outside the high-risk groups of sex workers and injecting drug users. Thailand became a model for other countries, illustrating sound public health interventions that included leadership commitment, multisectorial approaches within government, public education and aggressive intervention within vectors of transmission. Thailand's rate of new infection dropped dramatically.

Vietnam and Cambodia, in the grip of similar concentrated epidemics watched but were slow to act. In Cambodia, however, the rate of new infections has slowed.

Overall, the devastation in Asia could outstrip anything our world has ever known. Nicholas Eberstadt, professor of demographics at Yale University, believes that in less than twenty years 7 percent of India's population, 5 percent of China's population, and 10 percent of Russia's population will be infected with HIV. The trends are well recognized and follow a well-established pattern fueled by inaction, lack of government support and alarming increases in high-risk behaviors of injecting drug use and prostitution.

"Eberstadt projects that China will have more than 100 million new infections and 48 million deaths, India will have 140 million infections and 85 million deaths, and Russia will have 10 million infections and 12 million deaths. He believes that more people will die in China, India, and Russia than have died in all the countries of the world so far."[7]

The Golden Triangle, a lawless area of opium production where Myanmar, Laos and Thailand meet, is not just the global supplier of illegal drugs. There is also a strong local market. Injecting drug users find the same bargain prices for drugs as for counterfeit designer watches. Drug users share their needles and their infection with others who pass it on through sex.

It is easier to stop the transmission of HIV through the use of clean needles and through prevention than it is to rehabilitate those who are already addicted. Drug rehabilitation takes a long time and drains a great deal of resources. Addiction is a chronic disease, and addicts often relapse. But injecting drug use is a point of origin for the epidemic and must be addressed.

AIDS IN EASTERN EUROPE AND CENTRAL ASIA

At least three out of four HIV-positive people in Eastern Europe and Central Asia, like Olga of the Czech Republic, are younger than thirty years old.

> I am 18 years old. My name is Olga. I was taken ill of AIDS two years ago. I am in hospital. Why have you, you adults, thrown us under a tank? Why have you disrupted us with sex, pornography and drugs? You adults wanted "freedom," "relaxation" and "enjoyment." You approved pornography, wanted more money. You advocate "free rela-

tions," doing everything to satisfy your desires. But we are dying! We will not have families; we will not have our own children.

We are still alive, yet we do not live any more. You stole our childhood and our future too. We who are young and are dying do not know what real love is; we do not understand words like "shyness," "morality." The meaning of all these words has disappeared both from the schools and life too. You were taught their meaning and that is why you can live 70, 80 and more years. But we will die young! Four of my friends, used to be my schoolmates, have died already. Youth lie in mortuaries. We are burying each other already.

Why have you not warned us of your "safe sex"? AIDS and syphilis have become something as normal among us as flu. How grateful I would be now to the one who would have snatched the cigarette out of my hand, snatched the syringe away from me, who would have slapped my face for offering my body to others, talked to me about all this danger. Please help those who need your help now. Be open for those who are serving these young people.[8]

Over the last ten years the number of people in Eastern Europe and Central Asia living with HIV has increased twenty times to a total of 1.5 million, having increased by one third between 2003 and 2004 alone. More than half of these live in the Russian Federation and almost a quarter more (410,000) in the Ukraine. The governments of these countries have responded to AIDS as a medical problem with little organized attention given to prevention or to care. AIDS has reached a critical mass, and there is little in place to prevent an explosion that will devastate the youth of these countries.

The Russian Federation faces a huge AIDS crisis, with 940,000 already infected and a rate of new infections reported to be the highest in the world.[9] Hundreds of thousands of mostly young people are addicted to drugs, with many times more dependent on alcohol, and both these factors are accelerating spread, together with widespread ignorance, apathy and lack of resources. The challenge is formidable.[10] This is a nation spanning eleven time zones from China to Finland, where the average male life expectancy is already only fifty-seven years.

The epidemic in the former Eastern Bloc countries is driven mainly by drug users sharing needles. Many churches in Russia have been running drug rehabilitation programs for some years and have seen thousands of former drug users rehabilitated, often becoming part of the church. But now 40 to 70 percent of the people in these programs or who have recovered from addiction also have HIV. Growing numbers are becoming ill or dying, and children are being orphaned. Churches have members who are infected or unwell, many of whom are also recovering addicts, and pastoral care is becoming a major issue for them. In addition, churches are facing the need to support children who have been abandoned because they have HIV.

AIDS IN THE AMERICAS

The prevalence of HIV infection in North America is .8 percent, but it represents a health crisis for the African American community in the United States. Half of all new HIV infections in the United States are among African Americans who compose only 12 percent of the population. African American men are most likely to become infected through having sex with other men, while most African American women become infected through heterosexual relationships. AIDS kills more African American women ages twenty-five to thirty-four than any other cause, and is one of the three major causes of death among African American men the same ages. African Americans living with HIV or AIDS are only half as likely to receive antiretroviral treatment as other population groups in the United States. In 2003 twice as many African Americans as whites died of AIDS in the United States.[11]

The prevalence of HIV and AIDS is .5 percent in Latin America, and 1.6 percent in the Caribbean.[12] In six of the seven most populated countries in the Caribbean, the adult prevalence is higher than 1 percent. In the Bahamas and Haiti, at least 3 percent of the adult population is infected, and Haiti has the highest prevalence in the Western hemisphere (3.8 percent).[13] Over one third of Latin Americans infected with HIV live in Brazil, though prevalence is higher in Argentina, Colombia, Guyana, Peru, Suriname, Venezuela and all of the Central American countries except Nicaragua and Costa Rica.[14]

The pattern of HIV infection in the Americas follows several pathways. In Haiti, it is similar to that of sub-Saharan African countries where heterosexual spread is the primary means of transmission. The patterns in Brazil and the United States are similar to one another: Infection spreads outward through heterosexual relationships with partners from high-risk groups such as injecting drug users and men who have sex with men.[15]

As in other parts of the world, the personal crisis of being infected with HIV can present a life-changing opportunity. An American woman who had been infected by her drug-using former boyfriend and later married an alcoholic learned her HIV status through a routine prenatal test. In her pain, she cried out to the God she had heard about as a child in Sunday school. With the support of a caring church family, she and her husband have turned their lives around. Several years later, she is able to say,

Life is so much more peaceful when you let God be first in your life. I have been blessed with so much. I have watched my boys become Christians. I am so proud of what the Lord has accomplished through my husband and me when it comes to raising our boys. They are truly a gift. I didn't think I would live long enough to see my older son turn twelve years old. The Lord has blessed my marriage and my children. My husband has become my best friend. We have been married for ten years and he's been sober for seven. Another definite God thing! I have made many new Christian friends in my life. The Lord has given me his sufficient grace!

I have been HIV positive for fifteen years now. I don't have a perfect life, but I never will until I go home to be with the Lord. I just have a better life having God in the center of it. It is better because I don't walk around feeling guilty anymore. I know all I have to do is give my worries over to God and he will take care of them for me. I feel clean from the inside out. Sometimes I am grateful for HIV because it has taught me about what is really important in life. It has made me totally dependent on the Lord. The apostle Paul had a thorn in his flesh too. Second Corinthians 12:7: "And lest I should be exalted above measure through the abundance of the revelations, there was given to me a thorn in the flesh, the messenger of Satan to buffet me, lest I should be exalted above measure." Verse 10 says: "Therefore I take pleasure in infirmities, in reproaches, in necessities, in persecutions, in distresses for Christ's sake: for when I am weak, then am I strong" (KJV).[16]

African American churches have traditionally played a leading role in addressing health and social problems within their communities. Like African churches, however, they have been slow to respond to the AIDS challenge.

"AIDS is still a disease with a powerful stigma attached to it," said Martin Odom, pastor of St. James AME Church in New Orleans. "If you get cancer, no one says, 'Shame on you.' Unfortunately, we're not there yet with AIDS. I expect there may be some in my congregation suffering in silence or with family members suffering in silence."[17]

Yet, with few exceptions, in black churches "this is such a not-talked-about-subject. They're not going to educate anybody," said Michael Hickerson, a social worker who leads Brother 2 Brother, a support group for black men infected with HIV. Hickerson said he hears stories of a few infected black men who still attend church while guarding their secret. "With this epidemic, you don't have black folks rallying for other black folks with compassion, willing to care," Hickerson said.[18]

While the patterns of epidemics vary widely, there is a remarkable consistency to the personal experiences of suffering among those living with AIDS. And there are, in every place, men and women of great moral courage who lead in the fight against the disease that will most often kill them. Gracia Violeta Ross of Bolivia is one of these people.

Gracia's father is an evangelical church leader in Bolivia. She grew up in the church but, at the age of eighteen, decided to "live my life according to my will." In 2000 she discovered that she was infected with HIV.

Though Gracia became an advocate for people living with AIDS in Latin America, she held back from telling her church. She worried that they would reject not only her but also her father's leadership. Finally her father said, "If the members of the church do not understand this AIDS issue, it is because they do not have compassion. Then they are not real believers; they are only religious people. In case they reject you, it will be evident that they are not Christian." They *were* Christian.

Gracia recounts her experience: "I told them the truth and asked them as a church to forgive me because I offended God's sanctity with my wrong choices. The response was overwhelming; they reacted with love and support. They cried with my family and me for two hours. It was so amazing to see a routine-based church transformed into a source of love".[19]

WHAT WE CAN DO

The AIDS epidemic destroys those things that protect us. The HIV virus destroys our immune system. Stigma and death destroy the protection of intact families and communities. AIDS destroys the economies of families and even countries. The AIDS epidemic destroys health care as impoverished governments face the agonizing question of whether to provide treatment to those with AIDS or to fund primary care services. The devastation of AIDS is overwhelming.

Most of us can still visualize the images of Hurricane Katrina devastating the Gulf Coast of the United States in 2005. When the levees protecting New Orleans broke, every other protection—houses, possessions, employment, the belonging that comes from community—was also swept away. Americans responded with outrage against the apparent inability of anyone living outside the zone of destruction to grasp the scope of the crisis and to respond.

In Africa, AIDS has already destroyed the levees, and the storm and the flood are not abating in most areas. In Asia, Russia, Haiti and the Ukraine the levees have been breached and may yet fail. In the United States and the Americas, there is severe local flooding that has devastated entire neighborhoods but has not yet brought complete destruction.

Over twenty-five years have passed since AIDS made landfall and began its course of destruction in the world.

Our first challenge as Christians is to end the debate concerning whether or not we should respond to HIV and AIDS. We must instead repent of our slow response. After a period of time, a nonresponse becomes a response that eloquently communicates the state of our hearts and values.

Our second challenge is to decide how we should respond. The scope of possible involvement is just as broad as the scope of the AIDS disaster. We may direct our responses against the political, economic or social environment that continues to fuel the storm as we will discuss throughout the book.

We may be called into the teeth of the storm itself. But even there our responses may range from researching the biomedical nature of the virus to befriending someone infected with HIV. Even speaking of AIDS openly, accurately and with compassion weakens its stigma and power.

We may direct our responses within our own communities or outside of them. We should not all rush to Africa. Preventing the destruction of levees is in many ways better than rebuilding them. Intentionally strengthening those elements that protect against the spread or harm of AIDS is essential, even if it is never identified as an AIDS-related intervention. We strengthen the levees that protect us when we show restraint in our own sexual practices; have the courage to talk openly to our children, parents or friends about their sexual behavior; and refuse to participate in language or practices that dehumanize women, people of color, or gay men and women.

Our third challenge is to know with whom to respond. No single agency will be able to rebuild those physical, social, political and personal protections that were destroyed by Katrina. We who are Christians must join with all sectors of society to respond to AIDS. The fight against AIDS brings together many unlike organizations, divided by worldview and practice but sincere in wanting to protect and save lives. We as Christians often keep to ourselves, even though we may field highly effective programs. This is short-sighted. By withdrawing from the international and national communities of those who are allied in the fight against AIDS, we limit our impact, our learning and our influence.

Christians responding to AIDS are rarely asked to abandon or compromise their principles when relating to other groups to fit their efforts into a national plan. Increasingly, Christians known for their values and compassion are sought after by government and international organizations to be leaders in fighting AIDS and its impact. In Rwanda, Archbishop Emmanuel Kolini, the leader of the Episcopal (Anglican) Church of Rwanda, serves as the president of the National AIDS Commission, one of many church leaders throughout the world who participate in the context of broad national and international responses against AIDS.

When those of us who live in resource-rich countries finally begin to grasp the scope of the AIDS disaster, we ask, "How can we help?" That question comes from a God-given intuition, but our response is easily shaped by our can-do culture. Somewhere along the line, in our culturally shaped desire to help, we leap to the task of designing programs and strategies that will solve the problems that others face. We begin to think, if not to say, "With the right strategy, resources and commitment, we can lick this problem of AIDS."

We must remember that an AIDS ministry is more of a journey than a project. We can certainly walk with churches in Asia and Africa as they bear the burden of AIDS—as they have from the time the crisis began—but we must not try to take the burden from them and make it a problem that we will solve. We must sometimes stop trying to *do* something and simply listen. The process is guided not by rules but relationships. The time will come for projects, strategies and measurable objectives. But these plans and activities are sanctified to God's use through the relationships we have with our partners and with him.

Our final challenge is daily to pose questions like these: What attitude am I responding with? How vulnerable am I willing to become? Am I as willing to face the overwhelming impact of AIDS as Albertina, a church volunteer in Mozambique?

Maria greeted Joaquina and me (Deb) at the door and beckoned us out of the sultry coastal heat of Mozambique into the shade of her mud- and stick-framed house. We had joined Albertina and her partner on their regular weekly visit.

"How are you doing today?" Pastor Joaquina asked.

"Not bad," Maria answered.

Not bad? Not bad compared to what? The furniture was Spartan—one simple wooden stool and a rickety table, a single quarter-inch mat with huge holes. The still afternoon air sapped what little energy was left of the day. A small charcoal stove bubbled a broth of maize and beans for the evening meal.

"Thank you for coming. Here, please have a seat," Maria offered the stool to her pastor.

"How is José?" the pastor continued.

The story spilled out as Maria took us into the adjacent room to meet her husband, José, his younger wife, and her newborn baby. Everyone in the house—Maria, José, and his new wife and child—were infected with HIV.

Albertina, the church volunteer, started to serve—finding water to bathe those resting on the mat and asking questions about the baby's drinking, crying and sleeping habits. Every week, Albertina visits and cares for one to five families affected by AIDS. She is one of millions of Christians throughout the world whom God has called to visit and care for the sick. They are supported by their pastors and a cross-denominational group of churches that meet monthly in their own towns to guide the selection of volunteers, prepare them through training courses and support the volunteers' involvement in the homes.

But the work is tough. Volunteers receive no money, no reimbursement for travel on foot or by local transport. The heart cost is high—witnessing people in home after home on the edge of death, and child after child being orphaned. Volunteers not only seek to bring comfort, teach infection control and help relieve the responsibilities of family members, but they also seek to be the frontline extenders of Christ's compassion, counsel and presence in the shadow of death. For the AIDS sufferer, the journey is long, and the pain sears the soul.

The journey together may take a lifetime—not only for the person visited, but for the volunteer visitor. Many of them, like Albertina, are HIV positive themselves. They invest their energy while they have it as though they are making a deposit in a bank. They squirrel away perseverance and hope, knowing that eventually others will refresh them with their stores. Over and over again, the miracle of serving out of one's own suffering and giving out of one's own loss powerfully witnesses what it means to be a Christian. And Christ asks it of us all.

We cannot know Christ without knowing sacrifice. His calling is to all of his family, whether resource rich or poor, physically weak or strong.

TAKING THE NEXT STEPS

Personal Reflection

1. On a sheet of paper, list your talents, gifts and passions. Compare them to the broad areas of response required to address AIDS—science and medicine, social justice, advocacy and the political process, care and support, social issues, epidemiology and public health research, behavior change, economic strengthening, etc. Where is there a match? Ask God how he might want you to use the gifts and talents he has given you to address AIDS.

2. Jesus taught through stories. Read some of his parables in Luke. Now write a modern parable that captures what God is teaching you about your response to AIDS. (If you are not talented in narrative or storytelling, select another medium—song, dance, art, drama, poetry, etc.—to express your feelings.)

Action Steps

1. Find out about AIDS in your own community and the agencies responding to it. Your county or city health department would be a good

place to start your research. How significant a problem is it? Which population groups are most affected? Which community agencies address AIDS? What are the gaps in the response? How might Christians and churches respond?

2. The AIDS response is highly politicized on international, national and local levels. There is even the "politics of prevalence." HIV prevalence is the percentage of the population infected with HIV. In this book, we depend largely upon the estimates from UNAIDS. Research the question of prevalence on the web. Who are the winners and losers if prevalence rates at international, national and local levels are overestimated—or if they are underestimated?

3. Join a membership group such as Christian Connections for International Health (see resource section) through which you may relate to Christians from many disciplines and agencies who are involved in AIDS and other health issues. Begin to network with them via meetings and emails, to help you understand how you might respond.

4. Prepare a presentation on HIV and AIDS for your church, civic group or classroom. If you are a student, begin to write some of your research papers on AIDS and be open for God to speak to you through your research.

THREE

Finding Sanctuary

Just before sunrise, the religious leaders and their police entered the room. Startled, the man and woman inside broke their embrace. Surprise quickly descended into deep fear as one of the leaders yelled, "Man, is this your wife?"

The man jumped from the mat and grabbed his robe. Recognizing from the faces around him that a lie might well be fatal, he took his chance on a half truth. "No, but this woman seduced me. You have her. Let me go." The leaders said nothing but stood away from the doorway. The man fled, covering his face as he went.

They turned back toward the woman. "Put on your garment and come with us," they commanded.

As the woman began to adjust her head covering, one of the police grabbed it from her hand. "Whores don't cover their heads."

The leaders gathered their robes about them and strode from the room, careful not to touch the woman or anything else unholy or unclean. The police shoved her toward the door and through the crowd that had already gathered outside.

As the procession snaked through the narrow streets, already alive in the coolness of dawn, many, seeing what was happening, looked away from the woman and the leaders in disgust. Others, excited by the thought of a stoning, fell in behind, yelling abuses as they went. The woman's terror grew confused as she was led upward toward the temple rather than downward toward the gates of the city. She had heard that the very presence of God, the Holy Judge, hovered in the most secret place of the temple. But she also knew that if she were to be stoned, it would happen outside the city gates. At each turning, they continued upward.

The procession finally entered the great gateway into the court of the temple. They knew where to find the Teacher. Even before the leaders had burst into the adulterous chamber, their spotters had sent word that he was teaching in his usual place along the portico. This unclean Teacher, a friend of whores, had always outwitted them in the past. But those contests were the thrusts and parries of words. Words do not bleed and die. Whores do.

They had him trapped. The woman's guilt was unquestioned. The law of God demanded that she be stoned without delay. Whether the woman survived until sunset was of no real consequence. If the Teacher pronounced judgment and she died, the whispered message, "Remember the woman . . . ?" would destroy his following among many of the people. If the teacher excused her sin, they might even be able to bring him to trial. True holy men had the courage to follow God's law, especially when purity demanded a sinner's blood.

The Teacher's students fell back as the police set the woman in the midst of the crowd, facing the teacher. She collapsed to the ground as if she wished it would swallow her, but the leaders made her stand again, bareheaded and guilty, for all to stare at her shame. One of them put the question to the Teacher. "This woman is guilty of adultery, caught in the very act. Our law demands her death. What do you say?"

Some in the back of the crowd saw the Teacher disappear and began to wonder if he had collapsed to the ground. As they strained forward, they saw that he had not collapsed but had squatted at the foot of the woman and was writing in the dust with his finger. The leaders looked at one another in confusion and then back again at the top of the Teacher's head. Should they also squat before the woman to confront him? Instead they moved closer and hurled the question down at him again and again. Still he wrote quietly in the dust.

No longer the center of attention, and suddenly recognizing the exhaustion of her terror, the woman also looked down to the man who squatted so near her. As she traced the flow of his hair with her eyes, she began to wonder why she had been brought to him. Her fate hung on the word of this teacher who suddenly looked so small. What was he doing? Was he writing her fate in the dust that now clung to his fingernail as he traced patterns of letters she could not read? Or was he confused and trying to think of what to say? She wished that she could see his eyes, thinking they might tell her more.

Gradually the leaders and people grew quiet. The Teacher finally stood and brushed his hands together to remove the dust. He looked around at the people and fixed his eyes upon the senior religious leader. "Let the one of you who is without sin throw the first stone," he said.

Then he stooped once more and again began writing on the ground. The religious leaders searched their minds and one another's eyes for a reply. As each cast about in the labyrinth of laws and traditions that they had studied from childhood, each one slowly recognized that there was no reply to be made. One by one they quietly slipped away. This act of their morality play was now complete, and they had once again caught themselves in their own trap. The woman was of no importance now.

The remaining crowd asked one another, "What did he say? Why are they leaving?" Finally, as they slowly recognized that there would be no justice executed that day, they too, one by one and in small groups, drifted away.

The Teacher, still stooped down, looked about him. When he saw only the feet of the woman and the hem of her garment, he stood once more and faced her. "Woman," he said, motioning around him, "Where have your accusers gone? Is there no one who condemns you?"

Looking down at his feet, the woman replied simply, "No one, Lord." She looked up into his eyes again for his response.

"I do not condemn you either. Go on your way, but stop sinning as you have in the past."

(A retelling of John 8:1-11)

GRACE AND JUDGMENT

When the Pharisees put their question to Jesus, they could imagine only two choices. He would either have to uphold the law and condemn the woman or choose to preserve her life at the cost of obedience to the law.

When encountering AIDS, the church faces Jesus' choice. Because we know that some people who become infected with HIV have done nothing immoral to place themselves at risk, we feel compelled to ask the question, "How did he or she get it?" In other words, is the person guilty? If we discern sinful behavior, we then consider how we might distance ourselves so that no one looking on, including God, thinks we are excusing, condoning or even promoting sin.

Many who aim to hate the sin but love the sinner only accomplish the first because it is impossible to separate what people are from what they do. Instead we must simply love the sinner, that is, each person we have a relationship with. When we truly love people, we will have the right attitude toward the sin that affects them, but without condemnation. When we focus first on hating the sin, we will begin to premise our love and acceptance of people with AIDS on their presumed guilt or innocence, contributing to stigma for all who are infected.

Millions of people affected by AIDS throughout the world long to find a place of safety. Even those who have family and friends live behind masks of denial, hiding who they are and often the secret of their disease. Where will they find refuge? Will God's house be a safe house?

Sadly, many churches throughout the world have answered the latter question with a resounding no. They have chosen the pathway of condemnation, and become a profoundly unsafe place for people with AIDS.

Others have answered with a resounding yes but extend acceptance and love while totally ignoring issues of holiness when they arise. They feel that people with AIDS will not accept challenges to their lifestyles. They perceive that lifestyle choices are no one else's business and that churches have no authority to question them. The Pharisees had hoped that Jesus would simply excuse the woman so they could accuse him of ignoring the law and the holiness of God from which it emerged. Whenever we accept the Pharisees' challenge at face value, we fall into the trap they set for Jesus.

Jesus confounded the Pharisees by choosing both grace and holiness. He rejected their unstated but deeply held conviction that the two choices are mutually exclusive. There was only one person in all of Jerusalem that day who possessed the moral authority to condemn the adulterous woman. In bringing the woman to Jesus, the Pharisees had unwittingly also brought her to the safest sanctuary in all of Israel. Grace by definition is unconditional. Churches that answer yes to both grace and holiness become a sanctuary for those struggling with AIDS and also a community that invites repentance, extends forgiveness, and restores people to relationship with God and others.

In many Asian countries, homosexuality and AIDS both carry stigmas that result in virtual exclusion from society. Gay men with AIDS, then, risk almost everything of value to them by revealing either fact about themselves. A Christian setting in one of these countries provides sanctuary, a place where they may reveal and discuss both AIDS and homosexuality, which radically shape their lives and self-perceptions, without fear of condemnation and with assurance of confidentiality. When Jesus refused to condemn the woman in public and in private, he saved her from imminent death but also created a safe place in which she could hear instruction. The church's ministry of sanctuary includes all that we do to make AIDS more bearable and to lessen stigma. It may include care for families and individuals affected by AIDS, by caring for orphans, preparing for death, accessing treatment, or any other intervention in which the question of how HIV was contracted is immaterial.

Sanctuary was an essential aspect of Jesus' ministry. When he encountered the Samaritan woman at the well, he accepted the water that she drew for him and later went with his disciples to her town. His desire to drink from her water vessel and to eat with her neighbors signified perhaps more strongly than his words that he accepted them. His presence transformed a shared meal into a tabernacle in which even the despised were welcome.

Every time he touched people who were considered unclean, he profoundly reversed the judgment of the law that cut them off from worship and from their community. He restored them to far more than physical health. He restored them to their communities and families.

Like their Lord, churches too must embrace this mediating role. When churches model acceptance of men and women rejected by their cultures, they mediate their restoration to their communities. When churches begin to talk openly about AIDS and communicate through both action and word that people who are infected are welcome, they also become a bridge to greater acceptance within their wider community.

Grace is not contingent on behavior, but instruction, discipline and correction are. The church must embrace holiness as Jesus did. After telling the woman that he would not condemn her, Jesus did not say, "It's okay now. Just run along home." He identified her sinfulness and commanded her to change her behavior. While the woman was saved from imminent death, her life was radically changed. For the woman to leave her life of sin, she had to repent, seek forgiveness, reconcile to those she had betrayed, and slowly rebuild her life.

As Christians, we must address the behavioral issues related to AIDS. How we instruct and challenge a man who maintains sexual partners in each of his travel destinations will be different from how we counsel his wife.

The greatest challenge facing those of us who are involved in on-the-ground AIDS ministry is reflecting the convergence of grace and holiness, of sanctuary and correction. As we confront the tension inherent in this challenge, we will be formed into the image of Christ individually and collectively.

In over two decades of addressing AIDS, we (Deb and Meredith) have been transformed in ways we had not anticipated. We have resolved some of the dilemmas that we faced but still struggle to discern the way ahead in others.

Many readers of this book will also feel that tension. Some will become disturbed that we make any connection between sinful behaviors sometimes responsible for HIV transmission and the nature of our response. Others may sometimes wonder if we have lost moral direction in the maelstrom of ethical issues that whirl about AIDS. We hope that our experiences will frame a safe place for reflection so that God, through his people, becomes a refuge for those affected by this disease.

TAKING THE NEXT STEPS

Personal Reflection

1. When people blunder, bluster or otherwise enter into the zone of relationship surrounding you, what do they find? Is it a sanctuary where they can be themselves without fear of condemnation—a zone of safety and life—or is it a place of danger? Think of a zone of peace surrounding you as you go through the day today—a strong sanctuary where all who enter are affirmed in their dignity; not a place of rosy sentimentality or political correctness but where correction or rebuke may be heard without fear of rejection or comparison with others.

2. Reflect on those times in your life when even painful rebuke or correction has been helpful to you and those times that it has been destructive. What made the difference?

Action Steps

1. Over the next month, read through the book of Proverbs and note the verses that describe the power of spoken words for life and death, healing and wounding. Chapters 12 and 15—16 are good places to start. Read them often enough that they begin to influence what you say and how you say it.

2. From International Justice Mission (see resource guide) and other agencies addressing issues of social justice, find out how policies and practices of employment, immigration or inheritance systematically deprive people affected by AIDS of sanctuary. Join in some of the advocacy activities that they suggest.

FOUR

Protecting Our Youth

In Homer's *Odyssey*, Odysseus wrestles with the reality of confronting obstacles and challenges in life and of making choices that protect or destroy. "If man is given the earth to walk, then why did the gods put the stars over his head for him to ponder? And why do we have monsters to fight? And pirates and thieves? No, it is a puzzle that we are supposed to figure out, I believe, and these are the choices we have: to live our lives as men or slaves."

Choices are a part of life, and adolescence and teen years are a time when life choices are brought to the forefront. Youth decide aspects of their course of study, vocation, use of spare time, and the role of their friends. Adolescence is a period of transition from childhood to adulthood, most cultures marking it through rites of passage. In some cultures those rites may be the securing of a driver's license, being able to vote, finishing high school, or completing part of the spiritual journey of life and marking the milestone through church membership or perhaps communion or baptism. Some cultures celebrate initiation rites of circumcision or other mental or physical developments. Usually youth have cohorts who move through these phases of life with them. They deeply influence one another. In Africa this peer group, known as age-mates, develops strong relationships that include sharing privileges and responsibilities for the rest of life.

All youth experience rites of passage that are related to becoming a physically mature woman or man. For many youth there is experimentation with sex. In the age of AIDS, how this physical development and experimentation is controlled may determine whether youth are masters of or slaves to their bodies and minds. The choices they make may determine whether they live or die.

BAND OF BROTHERS

Tee is a typical seventeen-year-old in Phnom Penh, committed to friends and to having a good time. When school got tough, he dropped out and began scrounging for money full time, which most often meant sifting through garbage dumps for something to sell.

One of his friends invited him to join a group of guys to talk about life and learn something about handling love. Since Tee respected his friend, he decided to try it. The group of young teens and preadolescents met weekly in his own neighborhood, a stone's throw from the garbage dump where most of his daily search for income took place.

Riding his fifty-cc, Chinese-made motorbike, Raksmey, the adult leader of the group, coaxed the bike through the last few hundred yards of deep, hard ruts. He slipped off and propped it against the abandoned building in the center of the village. He lowered his backpack from his shoulders, pulled out a large blue plastic sheet and placed it on the ground. Ten guys kicked off their plastic sandals and sat down.

All eyes turned to Raksmey, who spoke to them. "Today, let's talk about something we all face. You see a gorgeous girl over there across the street, and you think she'd be someone you'd like to know. You find a way to finally get over there and talk to her, and you think she's pretty great. She seems to like you too. The next day and then the next week you talk to her. She's so beautiful you can't wait to have sex with her. That's all you think about when you see her and even when you don't. Anybody know what I'm talking about?"

"Yeah, we know. We're guys, right? That's just who we are. We can't help it."

The conversation was taken up by another member, Rith. Looking younger than his thirteen years, he pulled the centerfold from a pornographic magazine out of his pocket and explained that he found it in the garbage dump that morning. He was surprised and curious when he saw it. "Sure, the girl is beautiful," he said as he pointed to the picture. "But I don't do that yet."

A long discussion began. The boys spoke freely, talking about their relationships and fears. They asked questions that had been hidden deep within, connected to situations at home, what they thought about themselves, and their internal struggles with feelings and desires.

Raksmey continued his instruction, "You know, guys, this stuff we're talking about—sex—God actually designed. He made it for a man and woman to enjoy without reserve. He wants you to enjoy sex too, but he put boundaries around it. He said there's a right time and there's a right person. He calls the boundaries the responsibility of marriage. Marriage is also a time when you can commit to supporting your wife and developing your family.

"Anybody here married yet, except for me? I don't think so. So let's talk about why those boundaries are important and how we can keep them, and for that matter how we can protect our own lives."

They talked about the choices in front of them. They learned of decisions made by young men in the Bible like Daniel and his friends. They heard that making the right choice might be unpopular and costly.

A bond of trust developed among Raksmey and the boys. Some of them were sexually experienced; others were not. Some were eleven, twelve or thirteen, others slightly older. They saw in their leader a man who enjoyed his marriage and sought to honor God in all his life.

Their discussions were open and direct. There wasn't another forum like it for them. They learned about conquering the temptation of sex before they were responsible enough to marry. They came with many questions: How do you get the girl you really want? What happens if I get a sore? What is AIDS? What will it do to me?

The weekly meetings under the shade of the vacant building were making a difference. They traded secrets and developed accountability. Through the transparency and trust of Raksmey, the boys saw they could make wise choices and stick to them. They began to challenge each other and hold one another responsible for the choices they made. They realized that temptations sometimes came from within and sometimes from without.

Tee went back to school, believing he had control over his own future and could move beyond his of lack of purpose. Another boy, Sareth, discovered a new family within the group when his father died of AIDS. Rith found a safe place to talk about his fears of AIDS and garnered courage to burn the pornography in the pile where he found it. The ten guys challenged each other weekly, probing deeper into their lives and figuring out ways to help one another. They completed a workbook together, *Choose Life,* that helped them unravel questions they had about their own bodies and sexually transmitted diseases (STDs) including AIDS. They wrestled with temptations and how to avoid them. In the process they matured as young men, handling challenges in their everyday lives.

YOUTH ON THE EDGE

The Guttmacher Institute reports disturbing data on youth and sex. In the developed world about three-quarters of young women become sexually active as teenagers. U.S. teenagers are more likely than those in Western Europe to have sex before age fifteen and to have multiple sexual partners. The sexually transmitted diseases of syphilis, gonorrhea and chlamydia disproportionately affect adolescents and young adults. Teenagers in the United States experience higher rates of these sexually transmitted infections (STIs) than teens in other developed countries. Because of early sexual debut and limited use of contraceptives, U.S. teen pregnancy rates remain one of the highest in the developed world; most pregnant American teens are not married.

In other parts of the world, millions of teenage girls are married. In some areas such as South Asia, marriages of girls younger than fifteen years are common, often to men who are much older and sexually experienced. This practice is seen as a way to protect men from HIV, but it places their young wives at risk of infection and at risk during childbearing at an age where their bodies are not fully developed. Studies from Africa also confirm that teenage girls are far more likely to marry than teenage boys. Young African women tend to have sex before marriage, with an average one-to-two-year interval between first-time sex and marriage. For African men, studies indicate the time from first sex to marriage averages five years.[1] Certainly, the young generation is at high risk for HIV transmission through sex.

Many factors influence youth and sexual activity. A study published in the medical journal *Pediatrics*,[2] tied exposure to sex in the media to increased sexual behavior among youth. Chief author Jane Brown of the University of North Carolina said, "This is the first time we've shown that the more kids are exposed to sex in the media, the earlier they have sex."

The researchers interviewed teenagers between the ages of twelve and fourteen about their sexual behaviors and then again two years later. They also looked at the movies and television teens watched, the magazines they read and the music they listened to. They analyzed the media to determine how often sex was presented. They found that the teenagers who were exposed to the most sex in the media (the top 20 percent) were 2.2 times more likely to have sexual intercourse than those with the least exposure to sex in the media (the bottom 20 percent). This effect persisted even when they controlled for prior sexual behavior.

The report said that teenagers "may begin to believe the worldview portrayed and may begin to adopt the media's social norms as their own. Some, especially those who have fewer alternative sources of sexual norms, such as parents or friends, may use the media as a kind of sexual superpeer that encourages them to be sexually active."[3] The results of the study should lead us consider how complacent society has become in allowing sexual messages in its homes.

Other factors influence whether youth become sexually active. Extreme poverty, war, migration and AIDS itself can destroy the family structures and cultural norms that protect young people from HIV infection. Where these safeguards are absent, stressed and destitute youth may find themselves engaging in survival sex, often fueled by drug use that can deaden the pain of their circumstances. Both put them at greater risk of HIV infection.

These facts call for an honest evaluation and honest answers to address teen sex and HIV risk. Teen sexual behavior is one reason many public health officials consider calls for abstinence to be unrealistic and even unsafe. Youth are having sex, and we must protect them. But not all youth are engaged in sexual activity. It's important to reach youth before they become sexually active so we can guide them in making the life-sustaining choice. It is also critical to call youth to refrain from sex even after they have become sexually active, encouraging secondary abstinence as it also dramatically reduces the risk of infection.

The crisis of AIDS demands we do all we can to return society to the biblical mandates of honoring God with our bodies and keeping his gift of sex for marriage. It's a matter of life and death. Opponents of abstinence for youth claim that abstinence programs ignore evidence that youth need information about sex and condoms to protect themselves from HIV. Yet there is evidence that youth can and will change their behaviors and that abstinence works.

The *Journal of American Medicine* released results from a ten-year study of youth in the Centers for Disease Control Youth Risk Behavior Surveillance System, using data from biennial surveys in fifty U.S. states. There was a welcome finding: sexual activity among youth declined between 1991 and 2001 by 16 percent. In the same time period, youth reduced their average number of sexual partners by 24 percent. Given opportunity, education and support, youth change their behavior and set patterns for responsible adulthood. Maintaining responsible behavior remains the challenge.

Choosing Abstinence

As youth pass physically into adolescence, they also confront choices about their bodies, their relationships and the responsibilities they will assume in life. To make wise choices they require both information and also nurture. In fact, they must prepare for these choices in age-appropriate stages before they reach puberty. If we wait until girls start their menstrual cycles and boys' voices deepen, we've waited too long. They may already be sexually active or preyed upon for sexual favors.

Our friend Emily's son was eleven years old, the age for circumcision according to ancestral traditions in their Kenyan tribe. This ritual signaled the beginning of manhood when a boy took his rightful place in the family and clan as a man. The family adapted traditions of the village, since they were Nairobi city dwellers, and had their son circumcised in the hospital. Emily's husband, Joseph, an elder in his church, together with uncles and the fathers of the other initiates, seized this moment to openly discuss the character and responsibilities of manhood, the meaning of sex, the changes their bodies would face, and the temptations their minds would struggle with. Each night, as the boys were secluded and healing from their surgeries, the fathers instructed them. They discussed girls, marriage, sex, the role of the man, and the expectations of being a faithful clan member, husband and, some day, father.

Families and churches in every culture celebrate many milestones in their children's lives—baptisms, birthdays, graduations, engagement and marriage. As parents, relatives and other concerned adults transform these transitions into teaching moments, they help the youth understand the pressures around them and the options they have for living as men or women, and enable them to master their own bodies, decisions and futures.

Through a program called Project 5:16, designed for youth in America, youth speak honestly on video about their relationships with parents and peers and about their own self-image. Through street interviews, comedic drama and group discussions, youth share their stories and their frustrations with one another. The project name comes from Matthew 5:16: "Let your light shine before men, that they may see your good deeds and praise your Father in heaven."

A series of questions draw youth into thinking about the choices they have and how they can help each other defeat lack of self-control to wait for sex until they are married. The curriculum uses peer-to-peer education coupled with action steps. Groups are encouraged to get involved in fighting AIDS in their own community but also in countries where AIDS hits hardest. As they learn about AIDS in these countries, they also respond to a challenge to help by raising money for orphans, home care and prevention of AIDS among youth much like themselves but in countries with limited resources.

One youth group from Maryland decided to take a weekend to talk openly about their own physical pressures to have sex and learn how to help each other stay pure for future spouses. They watched the Project 5:16 videos and discussed the questions and statements youth were bringing to other youth. During the weekend some youth committed themselves publicly to abstinence until marriage. Others realized that, though they had already become sexually active, they could draw on God's forgiveness and grace and return to an abstinent lifestyle. The group also developed a plan to raise money for the AIDS ministries of churches in Africa. The teens not only dealt with their own situation, they also put their energy and resources into helping others avoid AIDS.

Teens from the Way of Hope Church in Cambodia developed a Khmer dance troupe. Every Sunday after church they practiced for presentations at church and community functions, including events to educate people about AIDS. At these functions, the troupe not only danced but also spoke about their own lives and their dreams for the future. They encouraged youth to get involved in local abstinence youth clubs and to understand how to say no to sex. In addition, the youth group started a Big Sib program, pairing youth with AIDS orphans. The youth learned how to grieve with children, how to support them and how to dispel the strong stigma attached to AIDS. The program is hugely successful, helping orphans with their physical needs and also making them feel special and loved.

Another group of young people from Minnesota decided to become involved personally and traveled to join hundreds of young people in Beira, Mozambique, for a citywide youth march for abstinence. There was music, dance, testimonies and posters. The solidarity among youth from diverse backgrounds spoke clearly: as young people they want to live, and they want to keep sex for marriage.

PROMOTING ABSTINENCE

In many countries where AIDS is endemic, the future for youth is interwoven with economic instability and political upheaval. In Haiti, many thousands of youth have joined Brigade Anti-SIDA[4] clubs connected with their local communities and churches. Despite Haiti's protracted political instability, the clubs are growing. Youth are demonstrating an alternative to street loitering and violence through productive activities such as creating art murals, developing community projects and engaging in supportive dialogue about taking possession of their own futures. The rite of passage in Haiti means the right to take control of their bodies and their own futures.

Promoting abstinence as a means of controlling AIDS has become controversial. Many professionals in prevention assume youth will not abstain, and therefore must be armed with information about sexuality and condoms as the only truly effective intervention. Responsible sex in this context, they say, means knowing yourself and accepting your sexual drive and the right to sexual expression, while protecting yourself and others. In fact, however, on any given day more youth throughout the world protect themselves by not having sex rather than by wearing a condom. The story of Raksmey and the teens in Cambodia illustrates the importance of investing in the generation that can be saved from the effects of AIDS through choosing to abstain from sex until marriage. It's an investment we simply cannot afford to *not* make.

In a panel discussion about AIDS prevention among youth at the 15th International Conference on HIV/AIDS in Bangkok in 2004, only one of the young panelists, a Ugandan, advocated the promotion of abstinence as a primary prevention strategy. He spoke about his own country of Uganda. Many of his friends were dying of AIDS because they engaged in sex outside of marriage. He decided he didn't have to die and chose to stop having sex. Many other young people were doing the same, making vows to not have sex until marriage and to support one another in that decision. "Sure it isn't easy. But I made a vow to myself, and I am keeping it." The results have kept him HIV negative and have contributed to the decline in new HIV infections.[5]

In the 1990s, Uganda decided it had had enough. Advances made in development after years of bitter dictatorships and war were eroding rapidly as Uganda's AIDS problem took root in most villages. The government and faith organizations brought a serious message: *You can change your behavior, or you can die from AIDS. You don't have to get AIDS. Keep to your own pasture if you are married. Zero graze. Don't roam. Stay at home with your wife or husband. Keep sex in marriage only.* The message was also clear to youth: *You can remain abstinent and live. And when you marry, have sex with your spouse only.*

The drive worked. Many thousands of youth participated, not only in wait-until-marriage rallies but in clubs and drama groups and accountability partnerships. It wasn't enough to talk about abstinence. They had to be part of an environment with others who believed self-control was possible, who supported and reinforced it. Such supportive environments had been traditionally African, developed for periods of initiation and rites of passage, but they had been lost with urbanization and other changes in their cultures. Eventually most people assumed youth would not take responsibility for their sex drives.

Through Choose Life, an AIDS prevention program that targets youth in Kenya, Rwanda, Mozambique and Haiti, youth and those who influence them learn about sex and support one another in their commitments to save it for marriage. Key points of the program's curriculum include

- Bodies are beautiful and worthy of respect and self-discipline.
- Friends may help or harm, so choose them wisely.
- Youth are sexual beings, just like everyone else, but they can take control of their behavior to avoid AIDS.

Parents, teachers and other community leaders need to be engaged in AIDS prevention. This includes not only educating but also modeling appropriate behaviors and fostering open and accurate communication with youth.

SUPPORTING OUR YOUTH

Outside an environment that supports sexual restraint, youth have an uphill battle. The media, the unfaithfulness in many marriages, and lack of clear and direct communication on appropriate sexuality all fuel the risk-taking nature of young people, making sex an easy option.

Loi, a Cambodian man, is facing the consequences of sex outside of his marriage and is now warning the youth in his country. Loi was a soldier in the Cambodian army, charged with discovering and controlling lingering pockets of rebellion. He was grateful to have a job and looked forward to returning to his wife in Phnom Penh when his tour of duty was over. During his military service, however, he was stationed far from her and rarely went home. But other women were close. Loi left his self-discipline at the entrance to the red-light district.

I (Deb) met Loi after his tour of army service when he was home with his young wife. Standing on the creaky floorboards of their living area located high above the flat flood plains, he proudly introduced his wife and newly born twin boys to me.

What should have been a time of celebration was instead a time of mourning. Loi and his beautiful wife, and possibly his boys, are HIV positive. The odds are that they will all die in the next few years. The one-dollar-a-night encounter with the sex worker cost far more than he ever foresaw.

Sadly he hung his head and looked at his feet for a long time, reflecting on his unfaithful behavior while away from his wife before he summoned the courage to speak.

"If only I had known," he said.

If only he had known. Our youth have to know *now*. Our strategies in youth groups and our instructions in homes and churches need to be fresh and relevant. Our hesitancy to talk directly about sex, whether within our marriages or as parents to children, contributes directly to our youth making uninformed decisions to engage in risky behaviors.

A group of concerned Christians in South Africa decided they had a responsibility to promote an understanding of the Bible that encouraged youth to look deeper into their own lives. They wanted them to make and keep decisions about abstinence that promoted life rather than taking away from it. For too long, South Africa did almost nothing about the seemingly distant brushfire of a rapidly advancing AIDS crisis until it consumed homes, families and entire villages. Today South Africa has the second largest number of people with AIDS in the world.

Teaming with the International Bible Society, South African youth pastors and other experts developed *Reach 4 Life,* an adaptation of the New International Version of the New Testament for youth in South Africa and other regions. This Bible and the accompanying program of discipleship are packed with straight talk about God's plan for sex and the temptations youth face in their world today.

One author of *Reach 4 Life*'s introduction writes, "I am in my twenties now and about to marry the girl of my dreams. We've been dating for two years and have experienced a beautiful, nonsexual relationship. She's an HIV-free virgin. Sadly, my sexual past—even from years ago—has broken her heart. But she is so grateful that I committed to wait since then. There's no emotional baggage in our relationship. The longer we wait, the more we look forward to the gift of sex! I want this joy for my friends—and for you."[6]

TAKING THE NEXT STEPS

Personal Reflection

How did you respond when you read the account of Raksmey in the first part of this chapter? What does your response, positive or negative, tell you about yourself and the cultural setting in which you live?

Action Steps

1. Evaluate the health risks and benefits of your own pattern of sexual behavior. If you are at risk, go for confidential testing for HIV and other sexually transmitted infections. Change behaviors that put you at risk.

2. If you are in a position to relate to young men and women in a family, work or ministry role, think through how you might address the behaviors that put them at risk.

FIVE

Ministry to Families

Ruth pulled her four-year-old daughter, Mweni, close to her bedside, turned her sightless eyes toward her and whispered, "Please come often to see me, Mweni. I miss you. I want to hear about your day and know how you are. Don't let the others keep you away from me. Come and see Mama every day."

Mweni hugged her mother and without a word slipped away to her aunt waiting at the bedroom door. She seldom returned to see her mother before she died. Her aunt and grandmother felt she couldn't understand and perhaps would get sick herself.

AIDS and its consequences separate families. Sometimes the separation is intended for good but is born out of ignorance or tradition as it was with Ruth. Too often the separation is for the rest of an ill person's life. Millions of children become victims of AIDS even though they aren't infected by it.

Families everywhere struggle to understand how to protect and help one another. Unfortunately, some believe that silence is the best option, protecting themselves and their families from shame and dishonor. But with silence comes great risk. Sometimes the silence is from ignorance: people infect their spouses without knowing they have the HIV virus. Sometimes the silence is rooted in hidden betrayals. Some are unfaithful in their marriages and put all family members at risk—a spouse through sexual transmission, a child through mother-to-child transmission, and children through orphanhood.

Advances over decades of improving maternal and child health are nullified by the toll AIDS is taking on women and children. Today in Zimbabwe, women have a life expectancy of thirty-four years, the lowest anywhere in the world for women, due to AIDS and Zimbabwe's deepening poverty.[1]

In Greek mythology, the story of Odysseus illustrates the stress couples face during physical separation. Odysseus traveled the world, leaving his wife, Penelope, behind. The journey carried him to faraway lands where he was lured by many temptations. On his journey home, when his longing for his wife was most acute, he was warned by the goddess Circe to be careful of the Sirens. Their enchanting music enticed men aboard ships that passed, luring them toward the arms of the Sirens.

Odysseus knew his weakness. He was intent on getting home to his wife and instructed his crew to strap him to the mast and put wax in their ears as the ship neared the Sirens' shores. As they drew closer and the temptation intensified, he commanded the men to tie him ever tighter.

Odysseus's ship passed the Sirens and continued home to Troy. His journey had taken more than twenty years, and his wife no longer recognized him. To be sure he was Odysseus, she challenged him to move their bed before she would enter it that night. Understanding the test, he declared it could not be moved because he himself had built it and knew it was part of a tree. Penelope had kept her marriage bed for the one who built it.

Many people are moving marriage beds. Vows taken to love and support one another for life are frequently broken. Proverbs warns us about adultery, "He who commits adultery lacks sense; he who does it destroys himself" (Proverbs 6:32 ESV).

The consequences of unfaithfulness are far reaching, bringing the potential for death not only to the one committing adultery but also to the spouse and their born and unborn children. What can we do to make our marriage beds secure and rooted?

BUILDING BETTER MARRIAGES

Preparation for a faithful marriage starts long before the marriage is consummated. As described in chapter four, our youth need accurate information about sex and AIDS. They need the guidance and role models of single men and women who abstain from sex and of married men and women who keep sex within their own marriages and who rejoice in the wives and husbands of their youth.

The AIDS crisis reminds us that marriages take work to stay healthy. Too often a healthy marriage is not celebrated or given the time and attention to *stay* healthy. We may make assumptions that our faith secures our marriage or that the love of our youth will always ignite a passion that protects. Reality may be very different.

Solutions to the AIDS crisis have to involve building better marriages. It's a life and death issue. Protecting a spouse and marriage means honestly confronting temptation and exploring ways to avoid giving in to deep and intense drives that are outside the boundary of marriage. How do we tie ourselves to the ship's mast to avoid the cries of the Sirens? How do we engage others whom we trust, like Odysseus's sailors, in our process? What accountability systems do we establish? How can the beauty of sex in marriage be rightly celebrated?

Some African churches face the challenge of talking directly about sex in marriage and building better marriages. Scripture Union, an organization originally oriented toward youth, saw the importance of building strong marriages so the parents of youth would be equipped to direct the spiritual and social development of their children. Their program, Aid for AIDS, teaches practical and culturally appropriate, and even culturally challenging, marriage enhancement at marriage retreats, including frank discussions about sex within the marriage context.

What can we do when our marriage beds are moved? Broken covenants need reconciliation. Pastors need training in counseling couples wrestling with broken trust and relationships.

A recently produced pastoral counseling manual, *Our Communities,* draws on more than ten years of experience by African pastors trained in biblical counseling principles applied to marriages and the AIDS crisis.[2] Biblical truth is woven into real-life case studies to provide practical guidance in basic counseling and reconciliation principles. Pastors attend one week of intensive basic training and then return to their parishes to apply what they have learned. After three months they resume training for more in-depth discussions of cultural and other complicated issues.

Not long ago in Africa, weak answers were being given in large church gatherings for how a spouse, violated by marital unfaithfulness, should respond. "Just pray and trust that God will protect you," a prominent women's seminar leader told a woman who asked what she should do to protect herself from AIDS because her husband was unfaithful. Surely God does protect, and prayer is important. At the same time, women in such situations—as well as their children—may be handed a death sentence if they aren't equipped with knowledge, negotiation techniques and communication skills so that they may speak with their husbands about marriage renewal, HIV testing and protection against virus transmission.

Strong families will live the Bible's call to celebrate and protect love. "You have captivated my heart, my sister, my bride, you have captivated my heart with one glance of your eyes, with one jewel of your necklace. . . . How much better is your love than wine, and the fragrance of your oils than any spice. . . . A garden locked is my sister, my bride, a spring locked, a fountain sealed" (Song of Solomon 4:9-10, 12 ESV).

CHILDREN WHO ARE LEFT BEHIND

As a global family, we will continue to feel the impact of AIDS for generations to come. Already fifteen million children have been orphaned by AIDS. Africa is hardest hit—eight out of ten children orphaned by AIDS live there. In some countries 17 percent of all the children are already orphaned, and the numbers are climbing.

Children are vulnerable to AIDS long before their parents die. Children in Africa are often the primary caregivers for their dying parents.

I (Deb) visited Sammy and his father, Kariuki, often. That was before Kariuki died of AIDS. Sammy was a teenage boy who normally would have been kicking a soccer ball outside or practicing algebra equations for his exam. Instead, he was washing dishes, going to the market, and emptying out his father's makeshift bedpan. It was unthinkable that he would be providing constant care for his own father, but there was no one else.

Sammy proudly showed me the neatly swept room and the clothes hanging on the line to dry before taking me to see his father, weak with fever and incessant coughing. Barely able to talk and nearly as thin as his walking stick, Kariuki struggled to sit up. Supported by Sammy's arm, he told his story, a story of abandonment by Sammy's mother, of reckless living and freestyle sex, of the loss of his steady job when he missed too much work, of the depletion of all his money. Sammy gave up school and friends to stay by his father's side. Too weak to work and too poor to get more help, Sammy's father had the family move in with Sammy's elderly grandmother.

I agonized over how to prepare Sammy for his father's death. It would not only mean Sammy would lose his father, but he also would become the head of the home. No school prepares a fourteen-year-old for that. We talked openly about the fact that there was no cure for AIDS and that his father was gravely ill. We tried to encourage him to find his uncles and other relatives to come and help him. Nearly every day a home care volunteer came to visit.

Sammy was with his dad the night he died. All at once he became the one to make all the household decisions.

For weeks the church volunteers visited Sammy, encouraging him to return to school and get on with his own life. One day when visiting him, I began to realize why he wasn't back at school. Sammy was deeply depressed. A photo album of him and his dad was in his hands as he said with his head hung low, "I wish I could have done more to save my dad."

Sammy felt not only loss but also guilt, guilt for something he only did right, never wrong. Sadly the physical needs of orphans are so many that their emotional needs are often neglected in the quest to secure education, land rights and access to food and health care. To address this problem, churches are helping families affected by AIDS to talk openly with their children to prepare them for the parent's death. Parents develop scrapbooks or stow away items in a memory box for their children to have after they are gone. They write letters describing their dreams for their children, thoughts about their lives together and often a prayer to include in the scrapbook or memory box.

Sammy is not alone. He has joined millions of children around the world who have lost at least one parent to AIDS. Asia, with its huge population, has the largest number of children orphaned by an array of causes—87.6 million—although the highest percentages of AIDS orphans are found in Africa.

UNICEF, UNAIDS and the United States Agency for International Development collaborated on *Children on the Brink 2004,* a handbook that highlights the issues for children orphaned by AIDS. This resource provides these key recommendations:

> The large majority of orphans and other children made vulnerable by HIV/AIDS live with a surviving parent and siblings or within their extended family, and the overwhelming thrust of an effective response must be to give direct substantial support to the millions of families who continue to absorb children who have lost parents. After losing parents and caregivers, children have an even greater need for stability, care, and protection. Family capacity—whether the head of household is a widowed parent, an elderly grandparent, or a young person—represents the single most important factor in building a protective environment for children who have lost their parents to AIDS and other causes. There is also an urgent need to develop and scale up family and community-based care opportunities for the small but highly vulnerable proportion of boys and girls who are living outside of family care.

Kenya's minister of state, Linah Kilimo, became an advocate for marshaling all community-level resources in the country, including Kenya's large number of churches, to help AIDS-impacted families. In February 2004, when *Our Children,* a manual to help churches care for orphans, was launched, she made the following statements about orphans in Kenya:

> No one knows exactly how many children are affected by AIDS in Kenya. We do know that AIDS touches all of us and that our children are impacted the most. Unless we act today we could have 2.2 million

Kenyan children orphaned by AIDS in the year 2010.

The church's guide, the Bible, is clear about our responsibilities toward orphans. In fact, it directly links the measure of our faith with
the practice of caring for orphans. "What is true religion?" James 1:27
asks. "True religion that God our Father accepts as pure and faultless
is this: to look after orphans and widows in their distress."

If every church practiced true religion, no orphan in Kenya would
go unnoticed or uncared for.[3]

The massive numbers of children who are orphaned sometimes invite
people to think of building orphanages. But, in the majority of cases, orphanages are not good for children. Traditionally, extended family members
have cared for orphans in concrete ways, taking in children with no parents
and providing them with basic needs of food, shelter and education.

I (Deb) remember visiting one orphanage outside Nairobi. The kind,
well-meaning woman who ran the home came out of her dwelling to greet
me. Several children, hair flying in their faces and tear tracks on their plump
cheeks, tugged at her full skirt. Another was propped on her hip. "Welcome," she said, as she began to share the history of her home as if it were a
well-rehearsed play.

The scene inside, however, was anything but well rehearsed. Hordes of
school-age children were busy at desks, and younger ones were scattered
across the floor. Kids were everywhere. It was overwhelming. This one kind
woman, assisted by her husband and a few staff members, was the primary
caretaker for over a hundred children.

Children need families. Africa's social structures have traditionally held
that children belong not only to parents, but also to the extended family and
the community around it. It is not uncommon for aunts to be called mothers
by their nieces and nephews, realizing that provision, discipline and guidance are also the responsibilities of the parents' sisters and brothers.

One of the most crucial concerns for children orphaned in Africa and
housed in orphanages or lost to extended family is an accompanying loss of

identity. Family and clan relationships and the land possession that often accompanies them are central to understanding identity and purpose. African theologian and philosopher John Mbiti states it this way: "The individual can only say, 'I am because we are; and since we are, I am.'"[4]

Without entitlement to land, a recognized family name and lineage, a homeland and language, orphaned children struggle to know who they are.

Orphanages are not the solution for children orphaned by AIDS. Yet they are often the first response rather than a last resort. Orphanages can never be a family, provide a secure identity or a place to belong. This is poignantly articulated in a letter sent to the Firelight Foundation by a fourteen-year-old African youth:

> I lost my parents to AIDS and then my auntie followed. I was then taken and adopted by an [orphanage] where I have lived for the last five years. I hate this place. It is an institution, not a home. I wish I was left with my poor grandmother, with just assistance for care. Today I have lost touch with most of my relatives. We live in homes named by numbers and so called house mothers. . . . We as children need real love from our relatives, not people paid to love us. . . . How can a child be adopted by just an organization?[5]

Children on the Brink also discusses orphanages:

> Orphanages, children's villages, or other group residential facilities may seem a logical response to growing orphan populations. In fact, this approach can impede the development of national solutions for orphans and other vulnerable children. Such institutions may be appealing because they can provide food, clothing, and education, but they generally fail to meet young people's emotional and psychological needs. This failure, and its long-term ramifications, supports the conclusion of a study in Zimbabwe that countries—and children—are better served by programs that "keep children with the community, surrounded by leaders and peers they know and love."

For children who slip through the extended family safety net, arrangements preferable to traditional institutional care include foster placements, local adoption, surrogate family groups integrated into communities, and smaller-scale group residential care in homelike settings. In some cases, a group of siblings may decide to remain in their home after the death of both parents. With adequate support from members of the extended family or community residents, this can be an acceptable solution because it enables the children to maintain their closest remaining relationships.[6]

Government policies in most countries in the world no longer include orphanages. Some nations such as Ethiopia and Rwanda have made remarkable progress in getting children who had been in orphanages during periods of war back into families. Care for the Children, an organization in China, is active in collaboration with national and provincial authorities in recruiting foster homes for many of the children now housed in orphanages. Their goal is to see one million children leave orphanages in the next several years, and they are making excellent progress by raising awareness in communities, actively recruiting and training prospective foster parents and guiding staff in local social service bureaus and orphanages to garner community advocacy, understanding and support.

WHAT THE CHURCH CAN DO

While the extended family is stretched beyond capacity in many communities (because of the death of several parents, aunts and uncles in the same family), much more can be done to keep families affected by AIDS together longer. Churches can prepare and support remaining family members who take in orphaned relatives and also support child-headed households through regular oversight of church members.

A movement known as Every Church, Every Orphan encourages churches in every corner of every town and village in Africa to join in the community care of orphaned children. The simple concept is that the responsibility to care for orphans and vulnerable children belongs to every church. In accepting this responsibility, churches become a catalyst to harness the traditional strength of the extended family and community to care for their own children. The program identifies a sense of urgency, broad scope and scale-up, compassionate acceptance of families affected by AIDS, and an open rejection of the stigma associated with AIDS and being an AIDS orphan.

Churches use their organizational structures and programs to contribute local resources to meet the spiritual and physical needs of families and children around them. They give what they have—love, skills, time, tutoring, mentoring, food from their gardens, material goods provided through church income-generating projects. Each church starts by identifying every orphan within a five-kilometer radius of their church building. They set up a committee that helps track and visit orphans and determine their needs. Then they develop plans to engage the church and the rest of the community to provide food, advocacy and shelter. But they do not take children away from the things that shape their own identity or force them into an artificial group identity. Siblings are kept together, and extended family members such as grandmothers are better enabled to offer care.

There are practical steps that can guide churches, community groups and families helping orphans. *Children on the Brink* identifies five key strategies:[7]

- Strengthen the capacity of families to protect and care for orphans and vulnerable children by prolonging the lives of parents and providing economic, psychosocial and other support.

- Mobilize and support community-based responses to provide both immediate and long-term assistance to vulnerable households.

- Ensure access for orphans and vulnerable children to essential services, including education, health care, birth registration and others.

- Ensure that governments protect the most vulnerable children through improved policy and legislation and by channeling resources to communities.

- Raise awareness at all levels through advocacy and social mobilization to create a supportive environment for children affected by HIV/AIDS.

The advance and access of new treatment regimens for AIDS is a hopeful breakthrough needing vigorous support within governments, funders and community members, not only for the improved health of the infected parents, but so parental support is available for their children longer. A major strategy for helping orphans must involve action in legislatures and communities before children are orphaned—assisting in the procurement of antiretroviral drugs and overall health care as well as compliance with drug regimens. As infected and sick parents improve their physical conditions, they return to work and provide for their children. It's also essential to support the good nutrition necessary for ARVs to be effective to improve the strength and overall health of the infected parents.

Because AIDS kills adult workers, its impact is felt most by the very young and the very old. Orphans lack the love of parents, but they also miss out on the opportunity for skill development, education and resulting prosperity. The old lack the care and support expected from their children who have died of AIDS. Instead they raise their grandchildren.

Recognizing this, church members in Rwanda decided to experiment with a model of apprenticeship that paired children orphaned by AIDS with skilled workers in the congregation. A church committee overseeing the care of orphans organized the project, guided the selection of children who would benefit most from it and trained the adult workers to understand skills transference. Children were paired with carpenters and mechanics, for example. At the end of the training period, the youth were given a simple set of tools to help them to continue learning and working.

The AIDS epidemic is growing in China. Initially, it spread through the sale of tainted plasma, the sharing of needles by injecting drug users, commercial sex workers, and men who have sex with men, but now there are fears the general population is widely exposed, giving rise to frightening predictions of a substantial increase in AIDS cases.

In the Yueyang City Church in China, a training session for church volunteers was held to explain different ministries that churches can have to help families affected by AIDS. During the training, the church members were asked to think about preparing for death and what they would want their children to know before they left them. What would they say in a letter to their children to be kept as a legacy?

One woman got to her feet and said with great emotion and force, "I would write to my child and tell him that I am a Christian and why. The most important gift I could give him is the assurance and love of Jesus."

Youth in Cambodia came alongside orphaned children in a different way—by adopting them in a Big Sib program. Teens involved in weekly AIDS-prevention club meetings decided to get involved in their neighborhoods. In addition to helping families with AIDS by cleaning compounds or washing clothes, they made friends with the households' children and continued the friendships after parents died. They met with the children each week, took them out for special events, involved them in sports, helped them with schoolwork and listened to their concerns. At times they identified issues that increased the children's risk and helped them to overcome these challenges through advocacy and support. Through the Big Sib program orphaned children gained new family members who conveyed a powerful message of hope and accountability for many years to come.

The church must be a place of sanctuary, particularly for vulnerable girls. In many places girls are caring for younger siblings after the parents die and are unable to go to school themselves. They also may become targets to provide sexual favors in exchange for food or other provisions for the family. The church needs to be sensitive to the special needs of girls and be strong advocates for their protection and rights.

Because needs are beyond the ability of many extended families to meet, many international organizations are helping through advocacy, donated funds and life skill training. Some active organizations are Compassion, Food for the Hungry, Tearfund UK, World Concern, World Relief, World Vision and Viva Network. (See resources at the back of this book for more details.) Many hundreds of small community and church initiatives go unnamed in proposals or newscasts, but they are the champions of effective care for needy children on their doorsteps.

As never before, collaboration is needed to be sure services are provided to all children, not just a chosen few. Concerted efforts are given to discovering which organization is providing what services and what gaps can be filled with expertise or guidance from other groups. As one grassroots worker in Kenya put it, "None of us can do everything. All of us can do something." The many *somethings* at the grassroots level are making a difference.

MARCEL'S FAMILY

A hot afternoon in Mozambique found us (Deb, local World Relief staff and church volunteers) approaching a decrepit one-room hut that looked more like an abandoned playhouse from my childhood than a twenty-first-century family's home. The roof was caving in; the paneless windows and doors were falling apart.

We lifted the remains of the door from the threshold and entered. A middle-aged woman sat on the floor, cradling a newborn, with another tiny baby draped over her legs. A single bed hugged the mud wall, and a young adolescent boy, with a smiling toddler hanging on his neck, peered in curiously around the door.

Their story unfolded. Marcel was the grandmother of twins whose mother, her daughter, had died of AIDS just weeks earlier. Marcel's two youngest children, the boy and his young brother, were with her in the home, but her older ones had moved away to Maputo, the capital city. Marcel's husband, the twins' grandfather, had died of AIDS years ago, and Marcel herself was HIV positive. Before us were the faces of three generations affected by AIDS. We didn't yet know if the infants were HIV positive.

We learned shortly after we visited Marcel that she had died, leaving the fourteen-year-old boy to care for his two-month-old niece and nephew and his four-year-old brother. What gripped every church and community volunteer that entered the home to help shoulder these responsibilities was the sense of belonging and love that the family clung to. Later the family was divided up. Some went to a Catholic children's home, others to a relative. I can't help but wonder if that sweet-faced toddler is still smiling.

TATU'S STORY

People cannot forget the orphans that sear their souls. Reflecting on the perspective of life and the reality of death, I think again about Tatu, the young girl who touched the heart of First Lady Laura Bush.

As the afternoon sun stole through the wispy grass hugging the thatched hut, the First Lady met her First Orphan. I imagine that first moment of meeting was as still as the sunlight, like my own first encounter with the suffering of AIDS.

Tatu, whose name means "three," has had three catastrophes to cope with in her twelve years of life—the murder of her father during the Rwanda genocide and war of 1994, the death of her mother from AIDS in 2005 and now the responsibility of caring for her three siblings until at least 2022.

Laura Bush moved with determined steps out of the hut into the church. To the sound of singing and full-throttled drum, she took her assigned place at the front. The pastor rose to the podium to pray and for a long second the singing, the drum, the snap of twenty-five press corps cameras and the rustle of reporters' writing stopped.

We were in God's house.

The church is home to Tatu now. Pastor Augustin took her in when her extended family threw her out. The church is the home to the Good Samaritan support group helping one another cope with AIDS.

TAKING THE NEXT STEPS

Personal Reflection

1. In many countries a young woman who is married is often at greater risk of HIV infection than a sexually active woman of the same age who is not married. In what ways do the dynamics of marriages in your own community and culture place married men or women at greater or lesser risk than if they were not married?

2. Imagine that one of your best friends has just returned from the doctor and shared in tears that she has tested positive for a sexually transmitted infection that only her spouse could have given her. Over the next days, weeks and months, what issues will she need to address? Who will she need beside her as she walks through this hard time?

3. How do you feel about the implied message throughout this book that the behavior of men contributes disproportionately to the spread of HIV infection?

4. The authors maintain that orphanages should not be a primary response to children who lose their mother or father. How do you feel about their position? How would this affect your personal or church response to the AIDS crisis?

Action Steps

1. If you are married, discuss with your spouse those elements in your marriage that either raise or lower the risk of sexual or emotional unfaithfulness. Decide on steps to modify those risks.

2. Patterns of sexual behavior within marriage and the vulnerability of widows and orphans are affected by issues of justice and economics, and cultural patterns of power and gender relationships. Using the resources listed at the end of the book, explore at least one of these three issues in greater depth.

3. Churches, Christian organizations and community-based agencies follow a number of strategies (e.g. orphanages, child sponsorship, church mobilization) in responding to the increased number of orphans caused by AIDS. Evaluate these approaches and increase your own personal and financial commitment toward meeting the needs of orphans.

4. Discover what puts children at risk in your own community and the ways that you and/or your church may help.

Avoiding the Violence of AIDS

It was spring in Jerusalem. The warmth had returned to the stone walls and roofs of the city. King David was restless. He climbed the stairs of the palace to the roof. He wanted to be in the full sun. He looked over the rooftops of the city in the direction where his men were fighting far beyond the horizon. Some had been with him from the time he had been hiding in the wilderness from Saul. He knew many of them by name. They had served him loyally in many battles.

Movement on a nearby roof caught King David's eye. A woman appeared with a servant girl holding a pitcher of water. Her hair hung loose. The sun was behind David and illuminated the woman. He watched the servant girl pour water over her hair and begin to wash and comb it. The woman removed her garment. She was beautiful. As David watched her wash, he began to imagine his hands flowing over her body like the cascading water. She completed her bath, put a fresh garment on and left the roof.

David asked members of the court about the woman. "Her name is Bathsheba," they told him. "She is married to one of your officers, Uriah the Hittite." He knew Uriah. A good man. A competent and loyal officer. David tried to put Bathsheba out of his mind, but she slipped back in at every idle moment. He sent for her. Almost from the moment she entered David's presence, both of them knew what would happen. He had sex with her.

Later Bathsheba sent David a message. She was pregnant. David sent a message to Joab, his commander in the field, and asked him to send Uriah to update him on the campaign. David heard Uriah's report and then urged him to sleep at home before returning. If Uriah would just have sex with his young wife, the child could be his. Uriah did not go home but spent the night in a palace room. The next morning, David again encouraged him to go home to his beautiful wife, but Uriah replied that he would not go to his wife while his fellow soldiers were in battle. David tried one more time. He spent the day carousing with Uriah, trying to get him drunk, but not too drunk. That evening Uriah staggered only as far as the edge of the palace before falling asleep once more.

The next day, David sent Uriah back to Joab with a classified communiqué. He told Joab to attack the city at its strongest point and, at the height of the battle, to pull back all of the men but Uriah. Joab did as he was instructed. Uriah and others were killed. "When the king becomes angry," Joab told the nervous messenger (David was known to have killed the bearers of bad news), "be sure to add, 'And your servant Uriah the Hittite is dead.'" David did not kill the messenger but sent word back to Joab. "Don't be upset. The sword devours one and then another."

After Bathsheba's prescribed period of mourning, David married her.

About a year passed before Nathan the prophet came to see King David to declare God's judgment on his treachery. David repented, but he had already brought violence into his family and kingdom. All knew of his sin. A week later the son who had been born to David and Bathsheba died. Bathsheba conceived once more, bearing a son they named Solomon.

Not long afterward, David's first-born son, the crown prince, Amnon, fell in love with his half-sister Tamar. But Tamar remained beyond the reach of even the first in line to the throne. As a virgin daughter, Tamar lived in the king's palace and under his authority and protection. Amnon fantasized so intensely about Tamar that he became haggard and weak. His friend Jonadab helped Amnon plot a tryst.

One day Amnon put his plan into motion. King David, hearing of his first-born son's illness, came to check on him. Amnon asked his father to send Tamar to make some special bread for him. King David agreed, and Tamar came. Amnon watched Tamar's young body move in rhythm while kneading the dough. The sight of her was as good as he had imagined. After baking the bread, Tamar placed it before him.

Amnon ordered everyone but Tamar out of the room and lay on his bed. He asked Tamar to feed him with her own hands. She entered, tore off a piece of the bread and leaned close to Amnon. In his sudden rush of desire, Amnon grabbed Tamar. "Come to bed with me, my sister."

The fantasy dissolved. Tamar pulled away. She argued that he would ruin both of their lives—she would be disgraced, and he, the first-born son of the king, would be a fool among wicked fools in Israel. Trying to buy time to escape, hoping that Amnon would come to his senses, she begged. "Wait. Ask the king. He will give me to you."

This Tamar was not the woman of his fantasy. This flesh and blood Tamar had ruined his plan and perhaps his life. Amnon would have her anyway, out of hate if not love. He raped her. When he was finished with her, he told her to leave. She refused to go. He called his servant and ordered him, "Get this woman out of here and bolt the door after her."

Tamar tore her richly colored clothes—the clothes of a virgin—and walked away weeping, her hands covering her face. She fled to her brother Absalom, her life ruined.

Absalom waited for his father, David, to take action. David was furious but did nothing. How could one who murdered to hide his own affair discipline his first-born for rape? In dangerous silence, Absalom's anger, unabated by time, grew.

Two years later, Absalom avenged his sister. He invited all of the king's sons to the countryside to celebrate the shearing of his sheep. Absalom's men killed Amnon as he ate and drank.

After a period of exile, Absalom returned to Jerusalem. Over the next years, he saw the growing unhappiness of the people with the king and began to build his own power base. Finally he called together men from all over Israel and had himself crowned king. Shortly afterward he marched on Jerusalem. David and his entire household fled except for ten concubines who were left behind to care for the palace.

> Absalom took Jerusalem without a fight and moved into the palace. On the day of his conquest, he pitched a tent on the palace roof. There on the roof, the same place where years before his father had looked down upon a bathing woman and desired her, Absalom, in the sight of all Israel, had sex with his father's concubines. Absalom and his father never reconciled.
>
> *(A retelling of 2 Samuel 11-16)*

When the prophet Nathan pronounced God's judgment on David's adultery and murder, he said, "You struck down Uriah the Hittite with the sword of the Ammonites. . . . Now, therefore, the sword will never depart from your house" (2 Samuel 12:9-10). David drew the sword when he took Bathsheba and murdered Uriah. Sexual sin and the sword entwined to weave death into David's kingdom for years, bringing pain and loss to thousands who had no direct involvement in any of the events. The impact of individual sexual acts reverberated throughout the entire kingdom.

Could anything in the kingdom of David have kept the sword sheathed? Or, once drawn, was there anything that could have shielded his family and kingdom from its devastation?

In Africa, millions of private sexual acts have forged a sword of disease that has brought unutterable death and suffering to its peoples and nations.

Many throughout the world work to slow the progression of AIDS, enabling people either to avoid exposure to its violence entirely or, when exposed, to lower the risk of infection. It is the work of prevention. Men and women avoid the risk of infection through sexual transmission when they avoid penetrative sex or when two uninfected partners live in a relationship of mutual faithfulness. A vaccination against AIDS would be the best possible shield from infection, but a vaccination effective enough to apply on a massive scale is a generation away, probably further. The only other shield in the armory today is the condom.

A comprehensive strategy for preventing the sexual transmission of HIV is simple to remember—using ABC.

Abstain from penetrative sex.

Be mutually faithful to an uninfected partner.

Use a **C**ondom correctly in *every* sex act that carries a risk of infection, if you don't follow the first two strategies.

AVOIDING THE VIOLENCE OF AIDS

When David had intercourse with Bathsheba, when Amnon raped his half-sister Tamar, violence entered and made its home in David's kingdom. Understanding why these women were violated will help us understand the barriers to successful strategies of abstinence and faithfulness and how the challenges can be overcome.

Both David and Amnon lived in a cultural setting of power and sexual practice that encouraged their behavior. They both knew that what they did was contrary to the law of Yahweh, but that did not dissuade them. In the progression of sexual acts from David's relationship with Bathsheba to Absalom taking David's concubines, sex increasingly became an expression of power for the men and powerlessness for the women.

Of all of the women in these accounts, Bathsheba is the only one who had even the slightest hope of changing the outcome of her encounter. Is there any action she might have taken to dissuade David from his design? She would have risked much to deny the king his will since David's power was absolute. Her husband came or went—even lived or died—at the king's discretion. Bathsheba most certainly felt she had no choice but to submit.

Tamar was wholly under the authority of men and had no choice about going to Amnon's house. She did say no and said it loudly enough that others in the house heard, but she had no power to avert her rape. In her case, the question was reduced to a contest of physical strength, and she was no match for Amnon.

The king's ten concubines, left behind to keep the palace, were never even named in the biblical account. They had no power to object to Absalom's action or to any actions of their masters. They are never mentioned again.

All of the men in these accounts were sufficiently powerful to become ac-
customed to sex on demand with little concern for the consequences. These
powerful men expected the women to whom they showed their sexual favor
to feel honored, and certainly not to resist or refuse.

The incentives for women to submit were themselves strong. In a situation where famine was only one failed crop away, concubines and wives of
powerful men were less likely to go hungry. Access to a powerful man
brought advantage to the friends and family of his concubines and wives as
well. Bearing a son would bring honor and influence. By the time Solomon
was competing for his elderly father's throne, Bathsheba had learned to pull
the strings of power effectively. For a woman to give up power over her sexual behavior became a pathway to power in other areas of her life.

That formula did not work for Tamar. She was already a princess and ap-
parently a beautiful and spirited person. Her rape changed all of that. When
Amnon violently raped her, he also blocked her pathway to further favor
and, in that culture, stripped her of her future dignity and worth as a wife
and mother.

All of the men had friends who assisted them in their actions. Amnon and
Absalom both plotted their sexual and power encounters with friends and
advisors. David used members of his court to plan and carry out his adultery,
and, except for Nathan, there is no record that any dared gainsay him.

For any of these men to have chosen differently, they would have had to
overcome practices and beliefs rooted deeply within their own culture.

EMPOWERING PEOPLE FOR CHANGE

To promote abstinence and faithfulness successfully in the face of the AIDS
crisis, we must address startlingly similar factors that shape sexual culture.
An individual commitment to say no to premarital sex or to partners outside
of marriage is often not adequate; our interventions must address the values
that shape behavior, not just the individual actions.

Few values, beliefs and practices are so firmly rooted in culture than
those that shape sexual behavior and relationships. To be effective in chang-

ing sexual behavior or the values and beliefs that shape it, a curriculum that has been developed for Rwanda cannot simply be translated into Chinese or English and used in Shanghai or Baltimore. A number of factors increase effective change:

First, begin with children. Waiting until a child reaches puberty to build the foundations for abstinence and faithfulness is waiting a decade too long. The beliefs such as "boys get to tell girls what to do" and "girls should do what boys say" are first shaped at the time boys and girls recognize they are different from one another. Children learn the patterns of gender power and relationships that they see and experience within their families and culture.

Beginning sexual education at the age of twelve is too late to reshape the beliefs and cultural practices. In many countries, over half of sexually active young adults act out what they learned in preadolescence, having intercourse for the first time before they are seventeen, men earlier than women. Effective preventative programs include a biblically based, culturally adapted, graded curriculum on sexuality in three stages—for children, preadolescents and adolescents.

Second, address behavior change as a process and not a single decision. A commitment to abstinence certainly does not ensure that it will be effective. (At least, not in all cases. A commitment card in Haiti had a place to fill in the duration of the promise. One young man, either honest or hopeful, wrote that he would commit to abstinence "until next weekend.")

Even though the stakes are high, the odds are stacked against sustaining safe sexual behavior. Young people are often surrounded by a culture in which sexual restraint is mocked or considered weird. In numerous places, abstinence strategies that urge young people, especially young women, to preserve sex for the bliss of marriage do not work. The models of marriage that the young people have observed revolve around procreation and unequal power relationships, certainly not something to wait for. Men who must delay marriage until they raise a bride price or establish a career in their late twenties and early thirties have to abstain through the years of their most intense sexual urges, something that very few can manage simply through personal resolve.

Securing a commitment to change is only the beginning of a long process. Maintaining new patterns of sexual behavior often involves the creation of lasting groups in which social support and pressure encourage people to remain abstinent and faithful.

Educators may unintentionally communicate that all is lost when a young person fails morally, or they may establish a judgmental climate that prevents a young man or woman from being restored without public shame and guilt. Those who have been sexually active or have had multiple partners must be welcomed to commit to secondary abstinence or faithfulness without the barrier of condemnation.

Third, help people know what to do and empower them to do it. All of the men and women in these biblical accounts probably knew what they should and shouldn't do in regard to sexual behavior. Tamar is the only one who tried, albeit unsuccessfully, to translate this knowledge into action.

World Relief's Mobilizing Youth for Life (MYFL)[1] team visited a high school for girls in western Kenya. Members of youth clubs who had made a commitment to abstinence presented a drama that they had created with the help of their teachers and peer educators. At the end of the assembly, the MYFL team introduced a new verse to a song that most of the 480 girls had sung since elementary school.

Head and shoulders, knees and toes, knees and toes, knees and toes
Head and shoulders, knees and toes,
Eyes, ears, mouth and nose.

They sang, touching the body parts as they were mentioned. But what about the parts of the body between the shoulders and the knees? The MYFL staff introduced a new verse:

These are my private parts, private parts, private parts.
These are my private parts; do not touch them!

As the girls began to do the actions, touching or pointing at their private parts, hilarity grew. In fact, the laughter and commotion grew so loud the teachers in the staff room came out to see what was happening. As the male teachers walked in to restore order, the girls insisted on singing the song twice more. Then they asked the male teachers to sing the song alone. As the teachers sang, the girls began to point to one of them and whisper his name to one another.

The World Relief team and everyone else in the room realized that through this raucous song, the girls were confronting a teacher who had abused or at least approached them sexually. They were also giving notice to the other teachers to keep their hands off. While the teacher was never officially reproved, the girls, by making his abuse public, stripped him of his power to harm them. The song became the national anthem of the MYFL program. Young women discovered that they collectively had power to confront their abusers, even when the abusers were in positions of authority.

Young men and women who wish to remain abstinent but who do not know how to resist social pressure often fail, not intentionally but because they lack the social skills to refuse sex. No individual person is likely to resist early sexual activity or remain faithful if everyone and everything are pushing them in the opposite direction. All people require social support—some group of significant people—to maintain difficult behaviors such as abstinence and faithfulness.

Women in many places of the world have little power in negotiating their sexual relationships, especially after they are married. In most African and South Asian countries, the majority of girls marry before the age of nineteen and often by the age of seventeen. Girls who marry in their adolescence are at significantly higher risk of HIV infection than sexually active girls who are not married.[2] The control that adolescent girls exercise over the sexual behavior of their husbands is little more than that of David's royal concubines. In most locations, when adolescent girls are married, they give up whatever legal protection they might have had while single. The same powerlessness is true of married women of all ages. Women are now more at risk for HIV infection than men and, for millions, their only risky behavior is having sex with their husbands.

Fourth, address transactional and transgenerational sex. Men exercise power in most sex between people of different generations (transgenerational sex) and sex in which there is some kind of transaction (transactional sex). The girls from the Kenyan high school challenged their abusive teacher collectively, something an individual student would have found hard to do. The teacher possessed the power of both age and position. He could reward the student who cooperated and punish the one who did not, often with little recourse for the student. Commercial sex workers do not drive most of the transactional sex in Africa. A woman may exchange sex for her food ration in a refugee camp, access to medical care, a scholarship, perfume or new clothes. Girls often seek out older men because they are able to offer more gifts, money and security than younger men.

Sexually active adolescent girls in Africa commonly have partners who are six to ten years older.[3] For adolescents, the rate of infection among girls may be several times that of boys who are the same age.

Preventative approaches and technologies are generally not under the control of women. Women do not control the use of condoms and often have little influence over the behavior of their partners. Female condoms and microbicides are two technologies women can control, but neither is in wide use.

Transactional sex is commoditized, commercialized and criminalized through prostitution and trafficking.

Chup Ly smiled at me (Meredith) in greeting, but her lips faltered as the sores hidden in her cheeks pierced her. In her uncertain smile I saw a ghostly shadow of her former beauty. I asked her to tell me the best thing that she could remember before her illness.

"I remember when I was healthy and without pain. I wore expensive clothes and was attractive to men." When Chup Ly was seventeen, her young body was healthy, full and well proportioned. Brothel owners in Phnom Penh paid her parents well for this beautiful young Vietnamese woman, but now they were demanding their money back. Their investment had gone sour. Even if Chup Ly were able to display herself, standing in a doorway, no man would approach her. Her silk dress hung loosely over her skeletal thinness. As our visit ended, a Vietnamese Christian prayed for Chup Ly. I reached out to touch her, consciously avoiding the spot of fresh blood on the right shoulder of her gown. I prayed too, but quietly. "Please, Jesus, help carry her pain."

After being embraced by hundreds of men who had sown death in her body, Chup Ly, in the quiet desperation of her sickness, had finally clung to the only man who had always loved her. In Jesus' embrace she had found not death but life. About two months later, Chup Ly, at the age of twenty-one, died and fled to the home of her true lover.

Chup Ly's transition into commercial sex is distressingly common. For her poor parents, paid sex work provided a source of steady income. Chup Ly betrayed no sense of shame in the choice of her parents for her. Like hundreds of young women in South and Southeast Asia, this work became her contribution to the welfare of her family. Over two million commercial sex workers service the men of India, and in Mumbai (Bombay) 60 percent of them carry the HIV virus.[4]

Sexual trafficking robs women and children of all power to lessen their risk of infection. Of the 600,000 to 800,000 people trafficked across international borders annually (this number does not include those who are sold or trafficked within their own countries), eight out of ten are women and girls, and half are children or adolescents. Most are trafficked into commercial sex.[5] Trafficking must be prevented by legal action as well as by enabling men and women at community levels to recognize schemes and protect their children.

Finally, empower individual moral choice. Many throughout the world have chosen to be faithful, to remain abstinent or to return to abstinence, especially Christians and people who practice other faiths seriously. Many people resist the predominant culture in critical areas of morality and practice. In Rwanda, World Relief asked some of the youth who had chosen abstinence to share the reasons for their choice. The fear of AIDS was mentioned by most of them, but it was not the strongest response. Many said that they chose to follow this difficult pathway to please God or to please their families.

The spiritual disciplines and the presence of the Holy Spirit in our lives protect us from sexual sin in ways that we are unlikely ever to measure.

Marckenzy is a young and energetic World Relief staffer in Haiti who serves as an officer in the local Anti-AIDS Brigade. In order to prevent his friends from contracting HIV, he also promotes a message of personal transformation and moral responsibility to Haitian young people.

"Everywhere I go, it's always a pleasure for me to talk about my choice to remain sexually abstinent before marriage," he says. Some ridicule Marckenzy's abstinence message, but others receive it warmly, leading to plenty of speaking opportunities at some of the nearly two hundred churches that work with the Anti-AIDS Brigade.

"In Haiti, sexual relations have become almost a normal thing among young people," he says. "But I tell those who want to listen to be strong and resist the pressure."[6]

When interventions that change the sexual culture and practices of a population find synergy with moral courage, the spread of AIDS can be slowed. Uganda has demonstrated this. Infection rates among pregnant women in sentinel mentoring sites in Uganda fell from 21 percent to 6 percent between 1991 and 2000.

The rapid decline of AIDS in Uganda largely preceded the increased promotion, distribution and use of condoms. Between 1989 and 1995, the number of young men aged fifteen to twenty-four who reported premarital sex fell from 60 percent to 21 percent. Young women paralleled that decline; in 1989, 53 percent had reported premarital sex, dropping to 16 percent by 1995.

Just over four in ten sexually active men of all ages had more than one sex partner in 1989; about half as many did in 1995. The percentage of men with three or more partners fell from 15 percent to 3 percent during the same period. The percentage of women with multiple sex partners was cut by more than half, declining from 23 percent to 9 percent during the same six years.

In 1989 only 1 percent of Ugandan women reported ever using a condom, growing to 6 percent in 1996 and 16 percent in 2000. In 1996, 16 percent of Ugandan men reported ever using a condom, increasing to 40 percent by the year 2000. Relatively few of these men and women would have used a condom with every act of sexual intercourse.

The Ugandan AIDS strategy during this period was largely homegrown. These changes happened within a national context that was unique. In 1989 Uganda was only three years beyond the end of a devastating, bloody and unstable quarter-century under Milton Obote and Idi Amin. By 1989 the Ugandans were collaborating peacefully in drafting a new constitution. The economy was improving, and Yoweri Museveni was a popular and influential leader.

Recognizing the threat that AIDS posed to Uganda far earlier than most African leaders, Museveni began to talk openly and frequently about the disease, mobilizing all sectors of society to combat stigma, end discrimination, and support prevention and care. Behavior-change messages were culturally relevant, clear, direct and starkly presented as life-and-death issues. Sexual choices were clearly framed as moral issues. Clergy of moral courage told of their own infections and taught openly concerning sex. Museveni invested in testing and counseling centers and improved the treatment of other sexually transmitted diseases. In Uganda, AIDS prevention was transformed into a cultural movement for changed sexual behavior. People changed, and the prevalence of AIDS decreased.

WHAT WE CAN DO

We must begin with our own sexual behavior. Most who read this book live in cultural settings in which abstinence and faithfulness are ridiculed—a belief that is bolstered through the media on every hand. The list of questions to ask ourselves is long:

- Have I chosen to remain abstinent or, if married, faithful to my spouse?
- If sexually active outside of marriage, do I have the moral courage to repent and to change my behavior?
- Do I make myself accountable to anyone for my sexual behavior?
- Do I depersonalize my own or others' sexuality in my humor, conversations and attitudes?
- Do I view sex as power and conquest?
- Does my partner have a face or only a body?
- (For Christians) Do I worship Christ with my entire body or only from the waist up?

We then turn to our relationship to others:

- If I'm a parent, what do I model for my children by the dynamics of power and respect in my home?
- What lessons do my children learn from me about becoming a man or a woman?
- Am I willing to teach or to confront family members or friends about their sexual behavior?
- (For Christians) Do my church's leaders turn a blind eye toward the sexual behavior of its congregants or do the leaders confront, discipline and gently restore those who will repent?

Finally, we must ask ourselves if we really care about the structural forces that perpetrate violence among women, children and the poor:

- Do I care enough about AIDS to become informed?
- Do I care enough to advocate for international and national laws and conventions against trafficking?
- Do I care enough to become involved personally with those who suffer abuse?

- Do I care enough to consider a career that is bound up with the lives of the weak and poor rather than the powerful and wealthy?

The ABCs of prevention should also be promoted within the context of other AIDS-related interventions in order to be effective in society. To capture this broader context some agencies (such as Christian AID at <www.christianaid.org.uk>) have adopted the acronym SAVE:

Safer practices, including ABC;

Available medicines, emphasizing the essential role of accessible treatment;

Voluntary testing, reflecting the importance of HIV testing and counseling to mobilize behavioral change;

Empowerment through education, acknowledging that ABC is most effective only when HIV infection is destigmatized and people, especially women, have greater control over their sexual activity.

TAKING THE NEXT STEPS

Personal Reflection

1. Bathsheba is often presented in Christian teaching as a temptress. How have you thought of her? Reflect on the cultural and societal factors that shape our perspectives on women.

2. In what ways may a perspective of women as victims also be harmful?

3. Examine Jesus' relationship to Mary and Martha in these passages (Luke 10:38-42; John 11, 12:1-10). How did Jesus empower Mary and Martha to transcend and/or to fulfill with dignity and worth the gender roles established for them by their culture? (Martha is more than Mary's foil in these accounts—look especially at John 11.) In situations in which women have little power, how may men, who are willing to step outside culturally prescribed behaviors, empower women?

4. In what ways may churches contribute to cultural patterns of gender relations that place women at risk for HIV infection?

Action Steps

1. Using the resources of International Justice Mission (see resources) and related agencies, become informed concerning trafficking and active in opposing it.

2. Explore how the economic empowering of women may lower the risk of HIV infection.

3. Explore how the economic dominance of the Global North contributes to the conditions that nurture the spread of HIV infection in the Global South, especially Africa and South Asia. Consider how you might change your own patterns of purchasing and investment in response to patterns of structural evil.

4. Discover how you may be able to contribute to breaking the cycles of poverty and abuse that place people at risk for HIV infection in your own community.

5. Review the child protection policies within your own church. Do Sunday school teachers who suspect that one of their children is being abused know what to do? How do you screen volunteers in ministry with children? With which community agencies have you established relationships for referral of women who may be abused?

6. Whatever your position in the culture wars around issues related to AIDS, intentionally seek out, read and reflect on articles and books by credible authors with whom you would tend to disagree.

SEVEN

Shielding from the Violence of AIDS

The story of David did not end with Absalom. The first surviving son of David and Bathsheba, Solomon, wrote these words, perhaps reflecting on the experience within his own family:

> Drink water from your own cistern, / running water from your own well. / Should your springs overflow in the streets, / your streams of water in the public squares? / Let them be yours alone, / never to be shared with strangers. / May your fountain be blessed, / and may you rejoice in the wife of your youth. / A loving doe, a graceful deer— / may her breasts satisfy you always, / may you ever be captivated by her love. / Why be captivated, my son, by an adulteress? / Why embrace the bosom of another man's wife?
>
> For a man's ways are in full view of the LORD, / and he examines all his paths. / The evil deeds of a wicked man ensnare him; / the cords of his sin hold him fast. / He will die for lack of discipline, led astray by his own great folly. (Proverbs 5:15-23)

The Bible clearly teaches that men and women should remain sexually abstinent until marriage and then be faithful to one another as long as they both live. Though this ancient biblical teaching defines the most effective strategy to prevent the spread of sexually transmitted infections, this is not why it was given. The practices of abstinence and faithfulness protect and animate God's gifts of sexuality and sexual expression. Mutual faithfulness provides a firm foundation for procreation and family life. Regardless of AIDS or other diseases, Christians should practice abstinence and faithfulness and effectively teach them because they represent God's gracious design for our lives and families. As Christians, we need no other rationale than this one to promote abstinence and faithfulness.

Likewise, we as Christians are to avoid exposure to those elements of our cultures that promote promiscuity or unfaithfulness in marriage. This demands personal discipline, but it also demands that the church address those practices and values in any culture that violate homes and families.

Shouldn't the teaching of Christians and the church, then, end with the teaching and empowerment of abstinence and faithfulness? David's adultery and act of murder unleashed the sword of violence against his family and kingdom. Isn't this God's judgment? Wouldn't shielding others against that violence thwart the plan and punishment of God? Many in the churches across the world still ask these questions concerning HIV infection and AIDS. At the most extreme, some still proclaim, "The violence of AIDS is God's punishment of sin—a curse that he pronounces against evildoers. Without doubt the church and Christians should help others avoid that violence but, once it's unleashed, we shouldn't intervene or try to shield others from its impact." Others ask, "Isn't it destructive to admit to the possibility of failure in sexual restraint and to teach how to lower the risk of disobedience?"

Every intervention to prevent the sexual transmission of AIDS has both moral and practical implications. Practically, people who choose to expose themselves to possible infection have one remaining protection to shield themselves from harm—using a condom. Much of AIDS prevention is focused on shielding people from the risk of infection.

Morally, two values interact in AIDS prevention. The first is the high value that God gives to sexual purity, but the second is an even more basic value—the value of life. Effective AIDS prevention reflects the interplay of these two values.

Consider the interplay of these two values in the following contrasting examples: A young South African woman has unprotected sexual relationships with several young men throughout her university career, as does a young woman in the United States. Both have violated God's plan for sexual behavior. Both have placed themselves at risk for HIV infection and other sexually transmitted infections. The ethical dimensions of their sexual behavior are the same, but the ethical issues surrounding the protection of life are extremely different.

The risk of HIV infection does not depend wholly on behavior. It also depends on the percentage of people in the population who are infected and able to transmit the virus.

To illustrate, imagine two bags of marbles. The first bag contains 200 red marbles and 800 white ones. The second bag contains twenty red marbles and 980 white ones. A person is far more likely to draw a red marble from the first bag than from the second bag.

Because South Africa has a much greater prevalence of HIV infection, the South African woman is at far greater risk of HIV infection than her American counterpart, even though their behavior is the same. Shielding her from HIV infection becomes a moral imperative, driven by the value of life. Using a condom is the only effective shield against infection among those who engage in risky sexual behavior. (Even though the risk of HIV infection was low for the American young woman, the risk of infection from other sexually transmitted diseases was high. Though it was probably not an immediate issue of life and death, using a condom would still have protected her.)

SHIELDING PEOPLE FROM ACQUIRING HIV THROUGH SEXUAL TRANSMISSION

If a young man is intent on jumping out of an airplane, we should tell him about the parachute on the wall. A condom is in many ways like a parachute. It must be used correctly and consistently to be effective over the long term. A person who chooses to use a parachute for two of every three jumps will not make a fourth one. Latex condoms do not allow the HIV virus to pass through their protective barrier, but they must be used correctly (that is, not permit the partner to be exposed to sexual fluids) and consistently (in *every* penetrative sexual act). Men and women who use condoms consistently and correctly reduce their risk over time by at least 80 percent and probably more. (This does not mean that one in five of those who use condoms regularly will become infected by HIV. Instead, over time, they are four times less likely to become infected than if they had not used condoms. Only a small percentage of those who use condoms regularly and correctly will become infected.) The effectiveness drops substantially when condoms are used inconsistently or incorrectly.

A study of over seventeen thousand sexually active people in Uganda found that the 4.4 percent who reported that they used condoms consistently (no information was collected on whether they used them correctly) reduced their risk of HIV infection by over 60 percent. Those who used condoms inconsistently remained at the same risk of HIV infection as those who did not use them.[1] Another review of published studies showed that using condoms inconsistently reduced their protective effect to only one-tenth to one-twentieth of consistent use.[2]

Condoms prevent HIV infection. Condom use should be the primary intervention when the epidemic is concentrated among high-risk groups and has not yet spread to the broader population. In those circumstances, the use of condoms lowered the prevalence of HIV infection (see AIDS in Asia, chapter two). In contrast, for young people who are not sexually active, the priority in prevention is avoiding risk through abstinence. Even after sexual debut, returning to abstinence (secondary abstinence) or being faithful to one uninfected partner are the most effective ways for youth to avoid infection. Likewise, among sexually active adults, promoting fidelity with an uninfected partner is the best way to avoid infection.[3]

Regardless of which strategy takes the lead, all people at risk should have an understanding of all three elements (ABCs, see chapter six) of AIDS prevention. More specifically, all church leaders, pastors and youth leaders who are willing should be able to counsel about the use of condoms when it is appropriate. Youth and church leaders should have accurate information concerning condom use. A condom is often the difference between life and death for a sexually active person.

Condoms represent the primary shield against the sexual transmission of

HIV, but not the only one. There are other shields as well, which will be described below.

Treatment of sexually transmitted infections. Untreated STIs, especially those that cause open sores on the genitals, increase the risk of sexually transmitting HIV.

AIDS treatment. When the viral load of HIV (number of viral particles in a sample of blood) is decreased, the risk of transmission is also decreased. Sustained ARV treatment, then, reduces the risk of transmission. The protective effect of ARV treatment will be lessened if those being treated increase their risky behavior or fail to comply with treatment regimens (which also promotes the development of resistant strains of HIV).

Male circumcision. About forty observational studies indicate that sexually active men who are not circumcised are at two to eight times more at risk of HIV infection than those who are circumcised.[4] Circumcision carries some risk, so there have been no clinical trials to confirm this. Because circumcision in many parts of the world is a mark of identity with a religious or ethnic group, most policymakers hesitate to promote it as a preventive intervention. There is no evidence that male circumcision provides any increased protection to the man's partner.

Preventing injuries to areas of the body exposed to sexual fluids. Women and girls are biologically at greater risk from sexual transmission of HIV than men. The risk is compounded when the genital organs are not fully developed or they are scarred from female genital mutilation (female circumcision). Additionally some sexual acts carry a higher risk of injury than others. Because anal intercourse increases the risk of injury many times over vaginal intercourse, the risk of HIV transmission is also increased.

Alternative sex. Alternative sexual acts that reduce exposure to sexual fluids are often promoted among discordant couples (one partner is infected and the other is not), between partners who are both infected and among men who have sex with men.

Avoiding alcohol abuse. Heavy drinkers are at a significantly higher risk of HIV infection than others. Many drink in the belief that it enhances sexual performance, and some drink to intentionally reduce their *perception* of risk. Alcohol also reduces the restraint required to avoid risk, and heavy drinkers are far less likely to use condoms correctly and consistently.[5]

SHIELDING PEOPLE FROM ACQUIRING HIV THROUGH BLOOD TRANSMISSION

HIV is not only spread sexually but also through infected blood. The first step taken by most countries to prevent HIV transmission was to make sure that blood products were safe. Potential donors are screened, all donated blood is tested, and procedures for safe donation and transfusion are practiced. All countries have these precautions in place now.

Universal precautions. Universal precautions were developed within health-care settings to prevent the exposure of medical staff or patients to disease through blood or other bodily fluids.[6] These precautions are applied to all patients in all settings. Anyone encountering bodily fluids that might contain HIV or other infectious agents avoids exposure by always using barriers such as gloves, masks and goggles to prevent direct contact. (Gloves and other barriers are used only when caregivers are exposed to fresh blood. To use barriers in normal interactions contributes to stigma and isolation.) Sharp instruments and other bloodstained items are thoroughly disinfected before reuse or are discarded safely. Disposable syringes have replaced reusable ones.

Universal precautions are also taught and practiced in workplace, school and church settings. Many churches train all their volunteers and staff in universal precautions and make gloves and other needed items readily available. All home caregivers should also be trained in universal precautions. In places where gloves are not easily accessible, caregivers can use other protection such as plastic bags.

Rites of circumcision; ceremonial tattooing, scarring or piercing; and traditional medical practices. Many cultures follow ceremonial, cosmetic or healing practices that carry the risk of blood-to-blood transmission. These must be modified to prevent exposure.

Sharing of needles among injecting drug users. Many injecting drug users share needles and thus bloodborne infections. Drug users also pass HIV to partners who don't use drugs through sex in exchange for drugs or money to maintain their addiction.

Needle exchange programs effectively reduce the risk of HIV transmission.[7] Injecting drug users who participate in these programs exchange used needles and syringes for sterile ones and are counseled about substance abuse treatment. Although needle exchange programs reduce HIV transmission, they catalyze intense ethical and policy debate. The United States, which has among the most restrictive policies and laws among countries facing the spread of HIV through shared needles, forbids the use of any federal funds for needle exchange. In many states and localities the possession or distribution of syringes without a prescription is itself illegal. Although no evidence supports the allegation that needle exchange programs increase the number of injecting drug users—or that they prevent drug abuse—they do protect against HIV and offer addicts an opportunity to enter substance abuse treatment.

SHIELDING PEOPLE FROM ACQUIRING HIV THROUGH MOTHER-INFANT TRANSMISSION

Without antiretroviral (ARV) treatment, an HIV-positive mother has about a one in four chance of passing the infection on to her newborn. Ideally, a pregnant woman who is HIV positive should receive a combination of medications throughout pregnancy to keep the level of virus in her bloodstream as low as possible. This can reduce the risk of infecting the baby to almost zero, particularly if she has a C-section before she goes into labor. For that to happen, the mother has to know that she is HIV positive by receiving prenatal counseling and testing and have access to this expensive medical care.

Because treatment like this is not available to most women in resource-poor countries, cheaper alternatives have been developed. Mother-to-child transmission of the virus is most likely around the time of delivery. Giving one dose of a single drug to a mother in labor and then to her infant within seventy-two hours of birth reduces the risk of transmission to 15 percent or less. Unfortunately, it also tends to increase the resistance of HIV to the drug that is used in this way, possibly making it less effective in the future.

The virus can sometimes pass to infants through breast milk, but breast-feeding is still the best option in areas without safe drinking water or an adequate supply of baby formula. In that case, the risk of death from waterborne infections (which cause severe diarrhea) or from inadequate nutrition is greater. Where breastfeeding is the safer option for HIV-positive women, it should be limited to the first six months until other foods can be given.

If pregnant women receive prenatal care that includes voluntary HIV counseling and testing, steps can be taken to protect their infants. For HIV-negative women, offering testing to sexual partners can help them to avoid becoming infected during pregnancy. Because of the stigma associated with HIV, women may be unwilling to be tested to encourage their partners to go for testing. The number of infants who acquire HIV at birth can be reduced through testing and providing access to simple ARVs, along with training on how to use them.

Most pregnant women in Africa still give birth without knowing if they are infected, without treatment and without even knowing that such treatment exists.

TALKING ABOUT SEX

When we (Deb and Meredith) first began to teach about AIDS to rural church members in China, our translator, a young married woman trained as a pastor, faced a major personal struggle the first time she had to use the Chinese word for *condom*. It was almost certainly the first time she had said the word in public and probably the first time it had ever resonated around the walls of the church. She survived, and the church building did not collapse.

Many of us come from homes where sexual matters were rarely, if ever, mentioned and, if they were, were spoken of in euphemisms. One adolescent girl asked her mom why a young unmarried woman in the church was pregnant. Her mom told her that the pregnant woman "had sinned." For a long time afterward, the adolescent girl worried that if she told a lie or was slow to obey, she too would wake up one morning and find herself pregnant.

To become involved in AIDS work, men and women must learn to talk about sex precisely and openly, but also with respect for this wonderful gift of God. Maintaining this balance in cultural settings in which sex is rarely discussed is a challenge that requires courage and sensitivity. When courage and sensitivity converge, preventive interventions won't introduce the uncertainty and misunderstanding that haunted the young girl.

We who are AIDS educators must guard our hearts and minds to avoid crossing the boundaries from frank and open discussion to depersonalizing sexual humor and sexual titillation. We must always recognize the power of our own sexuality and our own vulnerability.

TAKING THE NEXT STEPS

Personal Reflection

1. Which positions taken by the authors in the last two chapters have left you feeling angry, concerned or saddened? Examine why you have responded as you have.

2. In light of the biblical teaching to respect and preserve life, examine your own position on politically sensitive issues concerning condom use, needle exchange programs, and teaching alternative sexual practices that lower the likelihood of HIV transmission.

Action Steps

1. The "politics of prevention" are played out daily among policymakers, politicians, scientists, practitioners and people affected by AIDS. Globally and within the professional community, people may object to the use of ABC to summarize prevention strategies. Some object because it includes condom use, some because they see it as a U.S. policy with restrictions on funding and behavior change messages, and others because it does not explicitly include the context in which behavior

change interventions are effective. Because prevention touches on the most intimate of human behaviors, ideology and worldview inevitably become interwoven with behavior change approaches. Listen closely to the voices and evidence on every side, and take a principled and reasoned position based on evidence as well as Christian belief.

2. Evaluate the nature of education concerning sexuality and sexual practice in your church and community, and assess whether and how you may wish to become involved.

3. Read and consider the views of credible people with whom you disagree.

EIGHT

Providing Care

Swaddled in a boldly colored *kanga*, Ruth lifted her head slightly from the thin mattress as I (Deb) called her name. Next to her pillow was a cup of thick porridge, a picture of her daughter, and a crumpled cloth wet with phlegm. The open window over her head let in a welcomed swath of sunlight, igniting hope that perhaps daytime would bring relief from dark hours of labored breathing.

Ruth could not see me and strained to hear me. Extended coughing spells interrupted every few words she spoke.

"Yes," Ruth began. "I'm not afraid of death. For . . . for me . . . to live is Christ . . . and to die is gain."

Ruth is one of the 25 million people who have suffered through the long, slow process of dying, trapped in an ever-deteriorating body that no longer can fight debilitating illness. Antiretroviral medicines were not available in Kenya in 1994 as Ruth was dying.

New Medications and New Challenges

Three classes of antiretroviral medicines (ARVs)—entry inhibitors, nucleoside and nonnucleoside, reverse transcriptase inhibitors, and protease inhibitors—combat HIV at three critical stages in its replication. When used in different combinations, called "highly active antiretroviral therapy" (HAART), these drugs, under the best conditions, suppress the growth of HIV for years.

Almost every aspect of HAART is the subject of debate among policymakers, researchers, medical and public health practitioners, and even among people living with HIV. Access to therapy is determined by the treatment protocols and cost of the now over twenty-five different antiretroviral drugs on the market, the minimal criteria for entering treatment, and the availability of the clinical, testing, logistical and community services that support the therapy. Each individual patient shows different levels of sensitivity and resistance to the possible combinations of medicines as well as a wide range of tolerance of side effects. All of these change over the course of treatment.

Antiretroviral treatment now brings hope to many millions. Advances in drug effectiveness, affordability and availability are prolonging lives and in some countries transforming AIDS from an illness that brings death to a chronic illness that can be managed.

Eight of ten people who are medically eligible for ARV treatment in Argentina, Brazil, Chile and Cuba now receive it. The United States, Canada, Western European countries and some Asian countries also provide acceptable options for many or even most people needing treatment. Through hard-won battles the formerly silent throng of infected people in the hardest hit countries of Africa and in Haiti and India have now been heard, and great effort is being made to provide access to treatment.

But the vast majority of people infected with HIV cannot access the medications or the requisite medical care and follow-up. They may not even have adequate nutrition, which also prolongs life, or basic treatment for infections that can be controlled. The vast majority of those with AIDS, nine out of ten in Africa and seven out of ten in Asia, still have no access to treatment.[1] Even though the cost of first-line multidrug cocktails has dropped dramatically from over $10,000 to under $150 per year in developing countries, cost is one of the biggest remaining hurdles along with the lack of health facilities and personnel necessary for adequate care oversight across the lifetimes of the patients.

HAART, once a *cocktail,* an array of thirty or more pills taken at particular intervals throughout the day—in a sophisticated protocol of taken-with-food or on-an-empty-stomach—is now, in some countries reduced to a triple-therapy pill taken once a day. Pharmaceutical companies have made concessions in both price and cooperation, combining drugs from more than one company in the same pill.

Though short-term costs remain a problem for those millions of people earning less than a dollar a day, the long-term costs cast a much larger shadow on sustainability. Preserving access and assuring compliance so that drug resistance is controlled remains expensive. In 2002, the Malawi government allocated under ten dollars per person per year for all health costs including AIDS. UNICEF agreed in 2005 to provide the materials needed for ARV therapy—ARV medicines, medicines for opportunistic infections, and testing equipment and supplies—at a per-capita cost of $175 annually.[2] This does not include the cost of the staff or facilities that actually provide treatment. How will a seventeenfold per-capita increase in health-care costs for a single disease be sustained for the lifetime of those infected with HIV, especially as individuals survive the usefulness of the first line of treatment and have to begin more expensive protocols?

A government or donor agency that undertakes ARV therapy for people with AIDS also accepts a commitment to make it available and accessible for the lifetime of their patients. This is necessary for ethical reasons as well as scientific. Without drug maintenance, compliance and careful medical follow-up, drug resistance increases. In the natural cycle of treatment, the costs increase as individuals require second- and third-line medicines to remain in control of the virus. On a national or regional level, therapy that is interrupted by political turmoil, natural disaster or changes in donor commitment run a high risk of compounding the danger posed by HIV infection as the virus grows increasingly resistant to the least expensive therapies.

We have seen that ARVs support life and should be made widely available. Expanded treatment also poses new challenges to prevention. As infected individuals live longer, they have more time to pass the virus to others. While treatment reduces viral load and transmission rates, it does not eradicate the virus. In addition, the wrong perception that ARVs cure AIDS may encourage some to become lax in protective behaviors. Interventions to prevent HIV transmission must be aggressively continued and even increased.

Sadly, the hope of ARV therapy remains beyond the reach of most of the world's poor. Most of the people currently infected with HIV in the countries that bear the greatest burden of the disease will die without ever receiving ARV therapy.

Some individuals and churches ask if providing money for ARVs is appropriate. We certainly believe that sharing the resources we have to alleviate suffering, prolong life and sustain parents to care for their children are important and necessary. But one must count the cost and consider the long-term implications. Once treatment is started, it must continue for life. The issues are complex, and the assurance of proper care, supply and drug compliance are critical to success for the individual receiving the drugs and also for the welfare of those who become infected in the future. Our advice regarding ARVs is to advocate strongly for more access to ARVs and to start treatment programs not as independent providers but as an integrated part of a national government's ARV strategy.

Another important and more affordable aspect of care is the treatment of common infections in people living with AIDS. These simple medications do not stop the AIDS virus itself from doing its damaging work in the body, but they do bring relief and work to control or prevent the illnesses common to AIDS, such as TB and pneumonia. Even without ARV therapy, the rapid detection and response to these opportunistic infections extends life.

LIVING WITH THE HIV VIRUS

Regardless of access to ARVs, caring for people with AIDS and for their families and caregivers will never equate simply to treatment.

Hope at Home, a manual for home caregivers, outlines the basic elements of care for the person infected with HIV.[3]

First, you must know that people with AIDS can continue their normal lives as long as they have strength. That means they should continue working. They may have a small business at home to continue with. They can visit friends and go to church.

Sickness can come and go. At first people do not stay sick for a long time. They are able to do things they normally do. As long as possible a person with AIDS should continue doing their normal activities. They should care for themselves and their family.

Later people with AIDS will get sick and not get better. They become weak and thin. They might have diarrhea that will not stop. Maybe they will cough a lot. Many have skin problems. They will need more of your help.

Here are important things a person sick with AIDS must do:

- Rest when tired.
- Exercise by walking.
- Take the medicines the doctor gives them, especially the tuberculosis medicine.
- Drink lots of boiled water.
- Eat simple and good food.
- Take care not to pass HIV infection to others.
  - Avoid sex.
  - Use a condom if having sex.
  - Avoid pregnancy.
  - If pregnant, talk to your doctor about ways to avoid passing the virus to your baby.
- Always cough with the mouth covered.
- Cough sputum into a plastic bag or container and cover.[4]
- Be sure the room has windows and open them during the day to keep the air clean.
- Wash sheets and clothes and put them in the sun to dry.

People living with HIV and AIDS should continue their normal activities as long as possible, though this may not be easy. In areas where HIV infection continues to carry a stigma and there is no enforced legal protection in the workplace, the desire to maintain normal activities and work often conflicts with seeking treatment. AIDS-affected individuals might lose their jobs if they are discovered. When they seek treatment or are visited by an AIDS ministry team, they are more likely to be discovered. In Africa, cultivators or herders may become too weak to face the rigors of labor, and even entrepreneurs may find that people will no longer purchase from them or that all avenues to credit or insurance are shut down when their infection is known. Regardless of the country or place of work, HIV infection alters a life forever and necessitates compassionate care.

Jennifer was infected with HIV when she was young and unmarried. The shock overwhelmed her. She wrestled with the practical consequences of whether she should continue her job as a nurse in her home state of California and whether she would ever be able to marry. As she sought answers, she found kinship with others struggling with similar problems and connected with them through He Intends Victory (HIV), a ministry outreach to individuals and families affected by HIV and AIDS. Through fellowship, counseling and prayer she gained emotional strength. Her doctors put her on ARVs and monitored her progress closely.

Years passed, and her life took on new meaning when she met Rusty at church and married him. Together they pursued the next steps for ministry together and decided to venture to Vietnam where the AIDS crisis was gaining rapid global attention. They devoted themselves to building relationships, understanding the epidemic and seeking opportunities to train others. Jennifer's firsthand experience with AIDS gave her open doors that few others could have pursued.

Jennifer and Rusty's life illustrates important issues in caring for oneself and others who are infected. They committed to one another and pursued opportunities to minister to others through the uniqueness of their situation. They allowed themselves and their marriage to be vulnerable and transparent. In the process they were deeply blessed as they devoted themselves to serving their Lord together.

Herb also lived with AIDS and served through He Intends Victory. His ministry often focused on reaching out to men struggling with homosexuality and AIDS. A homosexual lifestyle in his early years gave him the virus, which he lived with for over ten years. He became a frequent speaker at support groups, churches, radio stations and international forums, sharing the testimony of his past life peppered with high-risk behaviors and his transformed life after meeting Jesus.

Herb attended every international AIDS conference and sought to be an influence among those angered by the force of the growing epidemic and the inability to find a cure. He made friends with some of the most far-left leaders of Act Up, a radical advocacy group. All who talked with him, even for five minutes, soon discovered his zeal for Jesus and his passion for seeing people affected by AIDS come to him. Herb died in 2004, but shortly before he did, he videotaped a message to be shown at his own funeral. He told those in attendance not to grieve. The agony of AIDS is gone, and he is enjoying new life with his Savior.

ESSENTIAL CARE

Lives, even of people who do not have access to ARVs, are extended by adequate nutrition, medications to control tuberculosis and ward off common infections, exercise, and a clean and pleasant environment.

In many places, people who become ill with AIDS live and eventually die in dark, stale and cheerless rooms, sometimes because they are hidden away or stigmatized, but often because poor people sleep in cheerless rooms and caregivers do not know care basics. Malnutrition may be rooted in poverty, lack of access to essential micronutrients or the inability to plow and plant land. Nutritional counseling given in the context of AIDS care often assists an entire family.

One association of people living with AIDS met every week in an Anglican church in Ruhengeri, Rwanda. Numbers grew and the association ministered to one another's needs. It was a safe place to openly share and to learn coping skills from others. When surplus U.S. grain was regularly distributed to the association along with thousands of other people living with HIV, the impact on their health was astounding. They returned to work in their fields, suffered from fewer common illnesses and resumed normal living—all because of ten kilos of maize and beans per month, per family. Sadly the project ended after three years, leaving the group urging for a return to one of the most basic treatments for AIDS—food.

Nearby, another project began a business venture of producing essential oils for the market. Although the project did not target people with AIDS, some participants are HIV positive and even those who are not help family members who are. The project, now in its third year, is scaling up following a successful pilot. It promises to not only generate income but also, in the future, to be a model for food production that particularly benefits families affected by AIDS.

Preventing infection from other diseases and finding rapid treatment for opportunistic infections is also essential. TB is a major threat.[5] One in every three people in the world is infected with the TB bacillus. Half of the people with AIDS will also contract TB. Twenty-one million people are coinfected with TB and HIV, and over sixteen million of them live in Africa.[6] People infected with HIV are more vulnerable to contracting and dying from TB than those who are not.

Malaria kills as many as three million people each year, and nine of ten malaria deaths are in Africa.[7] Because people with AIDS are often weakened, they are more vulnerable to dying from malaria. Sleeping under an insecticide-treated mosquito net is the best way to prevent malaria. People with AIDS also frequently suffer from chronic diarrhea, pneumonia, shingles and thrush, creating special challenges to those who give them care.

In helping people with AIDS embrace changes that will prolong their lives, we must also address fatalism. People who take action to change their lives are healthier than those who believe they are helpless. The diagnosis of HIV infection, poverty and chronic disease conspire to build a sense of helplessness among many who live with AIDS, preventing them from taking steps that enable them to live longer and better. AIDS workers no longer refer to individuals as *victims* of AIDS, but rejecting that word is more than an issue of being politically correct. Victims are helpless; people living with HIV or AIDS are not. God holds us accountable for our actions and has given us a gift of dominion—of exercising control over our own behavior and our environment. Christians ministering to people with AIDS can restore a sense of hope and self-efficacy that mobilizes change.

Caring also involves comfort. *Hope at Home* again presents it simply, illustrating care through photographs of people with AIDS and their families as caregivers.

Comfort is the gift that we can give to all people with AIDS. It means accepting each other. It means sitting with someone who is very sick. It means listening to them and talking to them. It means touching them.

Children bring comfort to their mother or father who is sick. Parents need the love and attention of their children.

Comfort means helping people who have pain. We can help a sick person change their position in bed to be more comfortable. We can rub their back with lotion. We can bring them something to drink. If the pain is bad we can buy medicine like aspirin or paracetamol to help take away the pain.

The family of the sick person also needs comfort. Comfort comes with talking together. It is important to talk together about family life and relationships. There may be problems from the past that families must talk about. Some may need to ask for forgiveness. This brings great comfort.

Families must make plans for the future. Together they can plan for the use of their family land or home. They must also plan for the future care of children.

The person with AIDS and the family need spiritual comfort. Reading God's Word, the Bible, and praying together bring comfort. God's Word says, "May the Lord of peace himself give you peace at all times and in every way" (2 Thessalonians 3:16). The visit of a pastor, priest, or church member brings comfort. All churches can help in this way.

The pastor or priest can help the person with AIDS prepare for death. Jesus said, "I am the Way, the Truth, and the Life" (John 14:6). Those who know Jesus are ready for eternal life. They have God's peace.

If you are caring for someone with AIDS, you also need comfort. It is very hard to see someone you love getting more and more sick. Talk to someone about this.[8]

THE CHURCH'S ROLE IN CARE

Caring for Chrub

Chrub could no longer shake off simple illnesses. She slept more and worked less. Her frame grew thin and her face gaunt. She quietly withdrew—from men, from society, from life. Even her mother no longer visited. Only her grandmother Sivon remained. Chrub struggled to eat, to bathe herself, to visit the doctor, to carry water. Too weak to climb the stairs to the main part of her house-on-stilts, she slept on the multipurpose platform below. People passed at a distance and talked about her in hushed tones. Neighbors were afraid to visit.

But Sukunthea, the church caregiver, continued to visit and began to bring others from her church as well. One started the fire and put on the kettle. Another went for water and began bathing Chrub. After drinking warm rice gruel and donning a fresh sarong and cotton top, Chrub pulled up a blanket and told her story. The women listened intently and promised to return and spend more time with her. They did return—daily.

God has uniquely gifted the church to respond to HIV and AIDS. The AIDS crisis paralyzes neighbors, who are afraid to get close, but it has finally awakened the church. Christians in Cambodia number less than 1 percent of the population. But as they reach out to people the broader community has rejected, they become a sanctuary of love that replaces fear, so hope is reborn.

Throughout the world, church caregivers—armed with an understanding of AIDS and the most basic principles of comfort, care and protection from infection—reach out into communities surrounding their church. They go from home to home, asking if there are sick people needing help. They do not ask about AIDS specifically to avoid stigmatizing the people whom they visit, but they visit all with chronic or disabling illnesses. When they find those who are seriously ill, they spend time talking and learning about their illness. Relationships of trust are built over a number of visits. If the sick person improves, the caregiver rejoices. When illness lingers and AIDS seems likely, the church members concentrate on helping the family understand the illness, go for testing and prepare for living productive lives.

Why is it that people with AIDS who come to Christ most often live more meaningfully than those who do not? In what ways does the Spirit who indwells them also bring life to their mortal bodies?

Some healthful elements of God's presence are captured in principles that have been well studied.[9] People with extensive social networks are healthier than those who do not have them. Brothers and sisters in the church often provide an alternative safety net for care. Like Sukunthea, they provide meals, clean homes, wash clothes, take people to the doctor and meet basic needs as they are able. Throughout these acts of service, they enter into close relationships with the families and individuals they are visiting. When churches extend full acceptance to those living with HIV and AIDS, they also combat the stigma of that disease among the wider community. They become mediators of community inclusion, bringing those with HIV and AIDS through the churches and into the broader community once again. Those who enter the valley of the shadow of death are more likely to emerge when they are not walking through it alone. Walking through hard times in the company of loved ones has a positive effect beyond the tangible helps that companionship brings.

People who enjoy close and intimate relationships with others are healthier than those who live with hatred or bitterness. People living with AIDS who are alienated from their families and communities must become reconciled to them to find true healing. God has gifted Christians for the work of reconciliation and comfort.

People living with AIDS are often starved for gentle touch. *Hope at Home* emphasizes the importance of touching people with AIDS.

AIDS also brings guilt and fear. Notifying a partner of one's infection status may damage that relationship. People who are living with AIDS must also repent or forgive, not because of the disease itself but because it most often emerges in the context of betrayed relationships. Christians, drawing upon the power of the Holy Spirit can help bring true repentance and reconciliation, not only to God but to one another. As relationships are made whole, the work of assuring a legacy to children and survivors can continue—not only by addressing their physical and economic needs but also by addressing emotional needs through memory boxes and scrapbooks. Items like these help children who have been orphaned maintain their identity.

Finally, a right relationship with God can remove the fear of death (though perhaps not the fear of dying). The sure hope of life with God after death enhances the quality of life before death.

People who find meaning in their suffering are better able to cope than those who cannot. God rarely answers the question *why me?* We dare not speak for him to one who is suffering. When we and those we love are suffering, we seldom discover meaning in answering the why questions. God chooses to answer our why questions with his presence, not with a reason. Those living with AIDS may find meaning in their disease when they discover that they are uniquely gifted to protect or help others. People living with AIDS often become advocates for change or walk beside those who share their pain. Or they may never discern meaning in their disease. People with AIDS often come together in support groups to share their journeys and minister to one another. Those who minister to others find strength for themselves.

The crisis of AIDS invites deep reflection on the biblical meaning of suffering, health and healing. Johannes Petrus Heath, a South African Anglican priest addressing a UNAIDS-sponsored workshop on theology and AIDS, said, "It's not only people living with HIV who need healing, but also the church. I believe that God has allowed HIV to heal the church, to force us to become Christian."[10]

People who suffer need relief, but so too do those people who live among the suffering. The church needs repentance for failure to act and from actions that have been self-righteous. The church needs cleansing from the hypocrisy of preaching faithfulness but sometimes living otherwise. The church needs to recognize its failure in guiding and supporting our youth toward abstinence and our marriages toward covenant keeping.

Matthew 25 and 26 record the account of Jesus during Holy Week, describing the walk of the righteous who will inherit his kingdom. They are the ones who give to him by giving to others—the strangers, the imprisoned, the hungry and the sick. Shortly after speaking these words, he went to the home of Simon the leper in Bethany where a woman anointed his head with an alabaster flask of expensive ointment. The indignant disciples, perhaps remembering Jesus' challenge to care for the physical needs of the poor and sick, rebuked the woman, announcing that the ointment could have been sold to provide something for the poor or sick.

Jesus' response was swift, defending the woman, "In pouring this ointment on my body, she has done it to prepare me for burial. Truly, I say to you, whenever this gospel is proclaimed in the whole world, what she has done will also be told in memory of her" (Matthew 26:12-13 ESV).

The message is clear. Our suffering Savior is at the center of ministering to those who suffer. As we give to others, our reward is not measured by acts of kindness, but by our devotion to our Lord.

As N. T. Wright reminds us, one aspect of Christian care transcends programmed strategies:

> What is our calling, then? We are called, simply, to hold on to Christ and his cross with one hand, with all our might; and to hold on to those we are given to love with the other hand, with all our might, with courage, humor, self-abandonment, creativity, flair, tears, silence, sympathy, gentleness, flexibility, Christlikeness. When we find their tears becoming our own, we may know that healing has begun to happen; when they find Christ in being held on to by us, whether we re-

alize it or not, we are proving what Paul said: God made him to be sin for us, who knew not sin, so that in him we might embody the saving faithfulness of God.[11]

Wright pictures the Christian stretched out painfully in a cruciform position, bridging the gap between God's grace and the suffering of the world. It is only when we are in that posture that suffering becomes sacramental, an authoritative sign that God's power brings life from death. It is only in God's capacity to suffer that suffering becomes redemptive.

When suffering entered the world through sin, God became its primary victim. We celebrate the suffering of Christ every time we participate in the Lord's Supper, linking our participation in Christ's suffering and death to new life and the freedom that life brings for service. *The Book of Common Prayer* speaks eloquently of the connection between Christ's suffering and our service:

> We celebrate the memorial of our redemption, O Father, in this sacrifice of praise and thanksgiving. Recalling his death, resurrection, and ascension, we offer you these gifts [of the communion bread and wine]. Sanctify them by your Holy Spirit to be for your people the Body and Blood of your Son, the holy food and drink of new and unending life in him. *Sanctify us also that we may faithfully receive this holy Sacrament, and serve you in unity, constancy, and peace;* and at the last day bring us with all your saints into the joy of your eternal kingdom.[12]

In writing this book we have struggled to communicate the pain of AIDS and often cannot find adequate words. In Romans 8, Paul also could find no words to communicate the intensity of pain that comes from living in a world of decay. There are only inarticulate sounds of suffering. The creation groans as if in childbirth to be liberated from decay. We groan inwardly as we wait for our full adoption as God's children.

This groaning would be meaningless noise, however, were it not for the

Spirit of God: "The Spirit helps us in our weakness. We do not know what we ought to pray for, but the Spirit himself intercedes for us with groans that words cannot express" (Romans 8:26).

It is not just we who are stretched between God and the world of pain. The Spirit, who is one with us, is stretched in that gap so that our groaning, mouthed or silent, becomes his. By his power and defeat of sin and death, our service and care to people living with AIDS is transformed from palliative treatment to true healing for all who discover Christ in us.

TAKING THE NEXT STEPS

Personal Reflection

1. Think through the following scenarios: (a) a gay young man, who had hidden his sexual preference from his family and church, receives notice that he is infected with HIV; (b) a young mother in Africa, who is infected with HIV, discovers that the last of the ARV medicines available in her country is no longer effective for her; (c) a young woman is dying of AIDS, and her younger sister is the only remaining family member who can care for her. What would characterize the suffering of each of these people? To which of them might God have equipped you to minister? Why?

2. Think back to a time when you or somebody that you loved was seriously ill. What questions came to your mind during that time? Who helped you or your loved one to walk through this period? Who, though perhaps well-intentioned, made it harder?

3. The authors maintain that sharing in the suffering of another in the presence of God may be sacramental, an action that becomes a special vehicle of God's grace. What do you think about that statement?

Action Steps

1. The poor in the global South still have very limited access to ARV treatment. Explore how the issues of social justice, international

patent rights, business considerations and corruption contribute to this. Read broadly and then take a position that enables you to become an advocate for the poor.

2. If you are friends with somebody who is taking ARVs, ask him/her to tell you what it is like, good and bad. Listen carefully and open yourself to the feelings that your friend expresses.

3. If you know of someone who is providing care to a person with AIDS (or anyone else who is chronically and seriously ill), explore how you, your friends or your church may be able to provide the caregiver with "time off" from their responsibilities.

4. Ask God for guidance in your ministry of giving for the care of people affected by AIDS. Do sufficient reflection and research to pick an area of AIDS intervention in which you wish to invest. Then choose an agency of demonstrated excellence (often requiring some personal conversations with staff and others) that reflects the priorities God reveals to you, and give sacrificially and regularly to their ministry.

NINE

AIDS, Sex, Sin and Forgiveness

In his book *Perelandra*, C. S. Lewis retells the story of Eve's temptation, setting it on Perelandra, the planet Venus. Weston, the tempter in the story, becomes the Un-man, whose humanity is consumed by evil. The hero, Ransom, is transported to Perelandra by servants of Maleldil, the true and good God.

The Un-man haunts the green lady who is the Eve of Perelandra, exploring the passions and longings that she has been given by Maleldil. Patiently and reasonably, the Un-man tries to awaken in her a conviction that Maleldil secretly longs for her to assert herself against his commands and walk independently of him.

When the Un-man is away from the green lady, he reveals his true character. In one striking passage, Ransom follows a pathway of eviscerated frogs to the Un-man, who is recreationally tearing them apart with his thumbnail and casting them aside. The Un-man longs to divert the pathways of life so that they lead to death instead.

AIDS, too, haunts the pathways of life, diverting them to death. God graciously gave men and women the gift of sexual expression as the most intimate celebration of life in relationship; it is also our joyful collaboration with him in creating new life. AIDS makes sexual expression a channel of death.

The womb provides the sanctuary in which a never-ending life is formed, and birth brings life into relationship. Breastfeeding nurtures early life in marvelously complex ways. AIDS makes the womb a place of infection, birth a risk, and breast milk a source of infection. HIV transforms blood, the very stuff of life, into the substance of death.

Ransom is deeply troubled as he observes the green lady's dangerous awakening to the Un-man's portrayal of self-assertive nobility. He engages the Un-man in debate, hoping to help the lady see the true nature of evil. The green lady, who knows only good, cannot fully discern the Un-man's lies. Ransom's arguments seem colorless and mundane compared to the Un-man's.

As Christians confront AIDS within the church, we find ourselves in Ransom's dilemma. Our first impulse is to detach ourselves from the pain, sweat, despair, betrayal and death of the disease. If we do anything at all, we engage with AIDS as Ransom first engaged the Un-man—in debate. AIDS is a scene within an ongoing morality play. Those who believe differently eagerly engage us, having us play villain to their hero in their version of the drama. We can easily be portrayed as sinning against people affected by AIDS by labeling their behaviors as sinful. Therefore we must know how sin, sexuality and AIDS are related.

Why does AIDS so easily catalyze an ethical debate? We no longer see leprosy as the setting for a moral contest. The diseases that kill most people in the global North are also linked to lifestyle choices that may be considered right and wrong behaviors. Yet these other diseases don't generate much moral discussion.

AIDS spawns ethical debate because HIV infection is most frequently transmitted by sexual behaviors that have a true moral dimension. Personal sexual sin drives the epidemic. But structural evil—the evil incorporated into the very structures of society, such as injustice, inequity, greed, racism or oppression—also plays a part, creating an environment that nurtures sin and multiplies its impact.

How then should we confront the sin that surrounds AIDS in ways that reflect Jesus Christ? First, we must have a clear understanding of the nature of sin and, more specifically, sexual sin. The Un-man understood that the temptation to sin is energized by desire for what is good. Sin is certainly expressed in thoughts and behavior, but the essence of sin is self-centered and heedless pursuit of those things that God already intends to give as good gifts. Eve sinned because Satan diverted her God-given desire for wisdom into disobedience. By Adam and Eve's disobedience they betrayed their intimacy with God and with one another. Temptation would have no power if it did not operate within the desires that God has given to us.

Sexual behavior is rooted in God-given desires for pleasure, intimacy, children and belonging, and the exercise of dominion or power.

Pleasure. God intends sex to be pleasurable. The anticipation, excitement and joy of sex animate the relationship of the young man and woman in the Song of Songs. The adulteress in Proverbs 7 also appeals to pleasure that will overwhelm all of the senses of the young man she hopes to seduce.

Intimacy. Intimacy is built upon the foundation of mutual respect, commitment and trust. The greatest respect one can show to the sexuality of another is to make and honor a lifetime commitment to exclusive sexual relationship. The trust that is built in mutual faithfulness becomes the guardian and builder of intimacy.

Children and belonging. Through conception, man and woman experience the joy of God in creating new life. In God's design, the intimacy of a marriage relationship radiates outward through interlinked generations of children to create the security, joy and identity that come from belonging to a family or clan.

Power. Through sex, people freely exercise the full physical, creative and emotional strength of their sexuality by bringing pleasure to another and giving oneself fully to a partner who will not betray one's vulnerability. Through abstinence and faithfulness, people intentionally curb the power of sexuality out of love and respect for another.

We sin sexually when we pursue God's good gift of sex without regard for his instruction. There are four patterns of sexual sin that help to drive the AIDS epidemic.

Pursuing pleasure without intimacy. That was great; you're way hotter than my ex. True love waits, sure, but who's to say that you can't have fun while you're waiting? Practice makes perfect, after all. Intimacy increases pleasure in countless dimensions. Risk, multiple partners, and the exploration of what's forbidden increase only two things: excitement and disease. Somewhere along the way, sex itself becomes insipid and only the quest for pleasure is pleasurable. Finally it all collapses into an emptied core.

Sex in the search for intimacy. *If you love me, you'll stay the night.* A woman who thinks that sex is the entry fee to intimacy becomes easy prey for men who want fun without commitment. She will move quickly through multiple relationships seeking the right man. Once she finds him, she'll not want to let go, even if he hits her. She may not walk away until she's tossed or carried out. Cynicism and bitterness germinate in the compost of abandoned relationships.

Procreation without intimacy or pleasure. *Yeah, I'd like him at home more, but at least he doesn't drink up his paycheck.* When procreation and sexual pleasure are separated, death and illness lurk at the door. The wife cares for the home, raises the kids and gives birth to new ones. The man has fun with his mistress or bar girls, returning home to impregnate and infect his wife. The "good" husband provides for the family, and his "good" wife keeps her mouth shut. Pity the wife who is barren. In many places she is easily cast aside and left to fend for herself, often selling her body to other men for their pleasure.

Sex as power. *Scored again!* Perhaps somewhere there is a *Book of World Records for Sexual Performance.* If so, each entry would have to appear in two versions. The greatest number of sexual conquests in a twenty-four-hour period in one version would become the greatest number of meaningless sexual humiliations in a twenty-four-hour period in the second version. A man might claim the prize in the first; a prostitute or gang rape victim in the second. In the game of sexual power, there are winners and there are losers. The seductress who entices the powerful man into her bed wins; the wife who confronts the betrayal of her most intimate relationship loses. King David wins; Uriah loses. Traffickers win; the trafficked lose. Whenever sex becomes conquest, competition or commerce, the weak lose, the strong win, and God is mocked.

HOMOSEXUALITY

Homosexuality became an issue in AIDS response because AIDS was first identified as a disease of gay communities. Gay and lesbian groups, energized by the number of gay men who were dying, became—and continue to be—vocal advocates for AIDS research and treatment.

AIDS became rooted among male homosexuals because their patterns of sexual behavior put them at great risk—not because God singled them out for punishment. Anal sex carries a high risk of infection because it is more likely to cause torn tissue, bleeding and condom failure. Casual sex with multiple partners adds to the risk. When gay men change their patterns of behavior, they lower their risk of infection. Two uninfected gay men who are mutually faithful to one another are at no greater risk of HIV infection through sexual transmission than their heterosexual counterparts.

Many homosexuals have the same desires for sexual relationships as heterosexuals. The movement within the gay community to become legally married is not simply an issue of power, benefits and rights. For many it represents a desire to express commitment, intimacy and trust within their relationships. Gays increasingly want the legacy of children and the belonging of family.

Because gays are driven in sexual relationships by the same goals, they also reflect all of the patterns of sexual sin that beset heterosexuals. Gay sex aggravates some of those patterns, however. Men take greater sexual risks than women, regardless of their orientation. When men have sex with men, the pursuit of sexual pleasure and adventure often trumps intimacy. In the United States from 1998 to 2004, there was more than a twofold increase in syphilis among men who have sex with men, brought on by an increase in their average number of partners and their number of unprotected high-risk sexual acts.[2]

How should Christians who believe that gay sex is itself sinful relate to those who practice it and minister effectively within a gay community? Some key principles must guide our response:

We must remember that Jesus more than anyone loves gay men and women without condition.

We must minister humbly, remembering that sin is common to all of us and that we are commanded not to judge or condemn anyone.

We must not accept the lie that sexual preference defines the identity of gay men and women. While we may reject that lie, we will encounter gay men and women who derive their primary sense of identity from their gayness. We must invite them into safe communities and congregations in which they are given dignity and accepted as image-bearers of God. When we can, we should help restore them unconditionally to community within their own families. We must name and affirm those marks of their identity, their gifts, talents or marks of character that are not derived from their sexual orientation, but from being made in God's image.

If we are working in AIDS ministry, we must focus on the demonstrated risks of sexual behavior rather than make moral pronouncements concerning it.

We must gently correct those who dehumanize gay people and oppose those who engender fear and hatred.

We must, as God gives opportunity, engage those who wish to repent of their behavior, referring them to people and organizations who can help.

STRUCTURAL EVIL

Personal sexual sin is by no means the only element driving the AIDS epidemic. AIDS also thrives in an environment of structural evil and injustice. Solomon was aware of an important connection long before the world knew of AIDS: "A poor man's field may produce abundant food, but injustice sweeps it away" (Proverbs 13:23). Injustice drives poverty, and poverty drives the AIDS epidemic.

A young woman such as Chup Ly (chapter six), who enters commercial sex work through the actions of her parents, complies because she knows that her family needs the money she can bring in. She may not fully realize, however, the forces that conspire to bring about their poverty.

Chup Ly's family was Vietnamese. They entered Cambodia illegally. The Vietnamese and Cambodians share a long history of mutual hatred. The barriers of animosity and illegal status kept them from joining the formal work force. All members of the family went out daily to find their food in Phnom

Penh. Some days were bad and others were worse. Cambodian men, however, enjoyed the beauty of Vietnamese women, who commanded a premium as sex workers.

Even if they had been Cambodian rather than undocumented foreigners, Chup Ly and her family would have been subject to the same forces of poverty that affect all the poor of Cambodia. Wages in the informal sector barely permit survival. The clothing manufacturers in the formal sector keep wages low to compete with other Asian countries in a world market. Most of the poor have no access to capital to build businesses of their own except through microcredit schemes, and even some of those are fraudulent or driven to maximize returns by loaning only to those who are no longer poor. Chup Ly's family members traditionally fished for a living, but, like most poor fishing families, could not find fair prices for their catch. The poor compete with one another.

Poverty is exacerbated by the inequities built into economic systems from the grassroots to the international level. Economics, not sex, drives the drug and people trades that compound the helplessness and desperation of the poor and fuel the AIDS epidemic.

A Predominant Culture of False Promises

Where there is sex in the city, there are bound to be sexually transmitted infections, shattered lives and identities, betrayed relationships and death. The costs of sexual freedom, however, do not make good television. The media—from MTV to billboards—daily unleash lies concerning sexual behavior to people living in the global North, who cheerfully and profitably peddle them to the rest of the world. In a Nairobi slum, men line up to pay for the worst in American television, music videos and shows that glorify violence against women and sexual humiliation.

A senior aid official in the U.S. government, who is a Christian, once confided that he was greatly disturbed when he discussed with members of the intelligence and military community why America gets such a bad rap in the Islamic world. As this Christian aid worker reflected on the long-term impact of entertainment exported from America, he found himself identifying more with moral concerns of the Islamic fundamentalists than with his colleagues. His colleagues perceived no danger in American culture.

When we (Deb and Meredith) met with Chinese university students to explore why they pursued sex so freely and with multiple partners, many (especially the women) replied that it was "to be modern." Sex was simply one of the accouterments of success, along with cell phones, a nice apartment and a well-paying position with an international company. They had bought into imported lies as readily as they bought designer labels.

When I (Meredith) travel, I have no problem turning down the propositions of commercial sex workers along the way. I know the dangers, of course. But the real reason is that I'm not willing to squander the precious riches of faithfulness and trust with my wife for what would be, in the end, an empty sexual experience.

I also live with the daily temptation that, with a click of a mouse or remote, I can immerse my imagination in a world of false sexual promises. I already share that temptation with millions of men and women around the world. Their numbers grow daily as temptation is exported globally. There is no physical danger involved in the click of a mouse or a remote. What stops my index finger is not the risk of infection from AIDS, but the knowledge that those who live in a world of lies will begin to shape their realities around that imagined world. With a click, I can dishonor my wife, myself and God. To do so is sin.

CONFRONTING SIN

OK, you believe in sin, but why make a point of it? Why not just keep it to yourself? Why do Christians insist on dragging sin into an understanding of sexual behavior? Is it not enough to talk about risk? What is the good in calling something bad?

First, it is simply more honest. AIDS educators may write, "Because older men drive transgenerational sex, we need to target them more deliberately with behavior change interventions." What most are thinking, in anger or sorrowful bewilderment is, how can older men prey upon young girls so mercilessly? Moral outrage in confronting AIDS is not evil. Any of us, Christian or non-Christian, who struggles with the consequences of AIDS, sometimes feels outraged—as we should. God has hard-wired us for moral discernment. While we may sometimes genuinely disagree on whether a particular action is wrong, we recognize that some things are clearly right or wrong. Our moral judgments shape our responses, whether or not we choose to acknowledge them.

Without a moral understanding of behavior we find ourselves in uncomfortable positions. If we persuade an older man to use a condom consistently and correctly when he has transactional sex with a high school student, is our job complete? Should we still try to change that behavior?

Second, in recognition that we all are sinners, we can minister with humility. How many of us emerge guiltless when confronted with God's instructions on sexual behavior—or in any area of life? When Jesus confronted the Pharisees over the woman caught in adultery, he destroyed their moral authority to condemn her just as he does ours. Only God can lay claim to the moral high ground. Only God, then, can judge and condemn.

Third, we are able to call people to sexual wholeness and not just away from sexual sin. God has given us a holistic model for good sex. It encompasses our relationships to one another, to him and with ourselves. Few would argue that long-term relationships of genuine intimacy based on mutual trust and faithfulness are unhealthy or wrong—though they may cynically question whether such things really exist. Christians and non-Christians agree on the risks that should be avoided or reduced in sex, but many non-Christians are hesitant to present a positive picture of what sex should be. In "sticking to the facts alone" they may portray physical acts devoid of intimacy and respect.

Finally and most importantly, without recognizing that sin exists there can be no repentance, no forgiveness, no reconciliation, no true healing. Early in the AIDS epidemic, the staff of MAP International (a Christian organization whose mission is to advance the health of people living in the world's poorest communities) in Kenya prepared educational materials and strategies. In designing the lessons, they looked for cultural bridges to understanding AIDS—things that were familiar within the learners' culture that could bridge the gap to new ideas. One especially hard concept to communicate about AIDS was that people became ill with an inevitably fatal disease as many as ten years after they were infected. The MAP staff conducted informal focus groups to explore this issue.

Only one cultural parallel emerged—a curse. A woman who had been cursed would probably not recognize the precipitating offense at the time that it happened. She would live under the curse for an indefinite time before it took effect, often in the form of sudden illness, injury or misfortune without an easily discerned cause. The woman and her family were able to discover the existence of the curse by looking backward in time, usually with the help of a *nganga* or shaman.

AIDS educators must fight the idea that AIDS is a curse, but the similarities between the progression of AIDS and a curse extend far more than the prolonged time between infection and illness. Most HIV infections, like curses, have their origin in the violation of a trust relationship. Most often, HIV infection is contracted because spouses or lovers break a bond of trust between one another. HIV infection brings other betrayals as well:

- The one child permitted to Chinese parents becomes infected while studying or working in the city, destroying the hopes and investments of his parents and shaming the family.

- Infected parents in Africa, who drain all of the family resources in treatment, leave impoverished children to already burdened relatives.

- The government or a health facility fails to screen the blood supply or clean instruments adequately, spreading AIDS through transfusions and procedures intended to protect life.

- As an expression of desperate community, injecting drug users infect one another by sharing needles.

Sin violates relationships. All sin betrays our relationship with God. We betray one another and even ourselves. All healing is movement back toward *shalom* or wholeness of relationship. AIDS ministries that do not address the restoration of relationships through repentance and forgiveness are incomplete. Repentance requires an acknowledgment that we have sinned. Ministries of reconciliation must be surrounded by prayer, and often involve sacramental elements drawn from church and traditional practice.[3]

Here is an excerpt from a simple home-care manual on AIDS that World Relief uses in Rwanda and other countries. Reconciliation is at the center of the narrative.

THE STORY OF JACQUELINE AND HER FAMILY

Jacqueline knew her husband was sick. He would not tell her what the problem was. As he got more and more sick, he knew he would die.

Jacqueline's husband went to the hospital for a blood test. He tested positive for the virus that causes AIDS. He was very upset. It helped for him to continue to work and care for his wife and six children.

There were some things he knew he wanted to do. First, he wanted to get legally married to his wife. He felt happy doing this.

He became more and more sick and could no longer work. He knew there was something very important still to do. He wanted to tell his family that he was dying of AIDS. He called his wife, family elders, and a friend to his bedside. He told everyone he had AIDS and that he was dying. He asked forgiveness from his wife. He told her he had been unfaithful and had sex with another woman. Jacqueline answered, "Thank you for telling me honestly what disease is taking away your life. May God make a way for you and may he keep you at His right side." One week later he died.

Jacqueline went to the hospital for a blood test. She is also positive for the virus of AIDS. She is using her life to help her children. She also wants others to know about AIDS.

Jacqueline permitted her story and photo to be included in the home care manual at a time when most people kept their infection a closely guarded secret, fearing stigma and rejection. Jacqueline wanted others to know the story of her family and their reconciliation.[4]

Understanding sin is essential to holistic ministry, but it also carries great risk. Calling something sin requires that we discern right from wrong. There is a great danger inherent in that process. When we recognize sin, we are inevitably tempted to condemn other people, especially when their sin, in our eyes, is much worse than ours. We forget so easily that there is no high moral ground that our behavior permits us to claim. When we fall into the trap of judging and condemning others, even indirectly, we alienate those we are called to minister to and with.

BUILDING A SANCTUARY FOR AIDS MINISTRY

In the climax of *Perelandra,* Ransom, seeing that the green lady is moving toward inevitable disobedience, pleads with Maleldil to intervene. Finally Ransom realizes that he himself is Maleldil's intervention. With terror and revulsion, he grasps that the battle for the soul of the green lady is not to be fought and won through debate. He fights the Un-man to the death. His battle is won in bloody and painful personal combat.[5]

The battle against AIDS also requires courageous emotional, spiritual and physical engagement. Lynne Hybels tells how Willow Creek Church is helping those who daily confront AIDS in their communities.

We were gripped by the plight of people devastated by AIDS, particularly in sub-Saharan Africa. Creating an ad hoc committee to begin a learning process, we read books, perused websites, and invited experts to teach us. We discovered how closely the pandemic is tied to broader development issues: education, employment, food security, pure water, as well as moral behavior and spiritual hope. We also discovered many African churches that are actively caring for the sick, providing food for AIDS-affected families, offering job training for widows, taking in orphans, counseling youth, and giving spiritual help. These congregations care for friends and neighbors in culturally appropriate and sustainable ways, but they work against great odds. It has been a privilege to learn from them how we can best encourage them. Thus far that has included leadership development and strategic funding. Because of the geographic distance we have been limited in sending serving teams, though we hope to expand that aspect of partnership in the future.

Previous connections in Africa through the Willow Creek Association and Christian NGOs [nongovernmental organizations] paved the way for our church-to-church connections, and continue to do so. We plan to expand our partnerships in South Africa and Zambia, and are considering a new partnership in Malawi.

For us, the greater challenge has been to educate and engage our congregation. How can we make the plight of Africans real to suburban Americans? We began by sending Willow leaders to Africa to capture on video the work of our partners. Building around these videos, we devoted entire weekend services to the crisis of AIDS, challenging Willow attendees to open their minds and hearts—and to give financially—to the holistic efforts of local African churches. We started monthly Learning Communities, bringing in experts to teach about HIV/AIDS as well as related issues of global poverty, holistic ministry, justice, and advocacy.

In response to the Willow Creekers who want to do more than "write a check," we have created AIDS & Global Poverty serving teams—volunteers who serve *Global Connections/Africa* through their expertise in marketing, administration, research, hospitality, prayer, and health care. Two of our newest teams are *Global Kids*, which develops creative ideas for families wanting to respond to global needs, and *Artists in Action*, a group of painters, sculptors, photographers, musicians, actors, and poets committed to raising awareness as well as funds for AIDS and global poverty. One *Artists in Action* plan is to create an image incorporating the names of one thousand orphans cared for by our church partners in Zambia, to serve as a visual reminder to all of us of the boys and girls who now have hope for a better future.

We believe it is equally important to engage locally with those infected or affected by HIV/AIDS. Through workshops and learning communities we are raising awareness about the needs closer to home, providing a support group for individuals and families affected by HIV/AIDS, and exploring partnerships with AIDS organizations serving in the Chicago area.

Jesus calls us to compassionate, intentional involvement in the lives of people around us who are suffering, stigmatized or marginalized. When such engagement brings us face-to-face with social or sexual behaviors we believe are not in line with Biblical teaching, we must carefully discern how to maintain deeply-held convictions without requiring that others share those convictions as a condition for our expressions of love. Jesus engaged compassionately and authentically with the woman at the well, drawing her into meaningful dialogue and addressing her primary need for living water. Likewise, we want to create an environment of safety and openness, where people in *any* kind of pain or need can discover the hope that comes from living under the shelter of God's love as mediated by God's people.[6]

THE HOPE OF CHRIST

So it is that Christians confront AIDS—in painful ministry. If people are to respond to the compassion and love of Christ, that compassion and love must become incarnate in the men, women and youth who compose his church. Christ's eyes are the crying eyes of the women who came to bury a woman who died of AIDS because no one else would. Christ's feet are those of the church volunteers who carry firewood to an impoverished widow in rural Malawi. Christ's anger is the anger of the lawyer who prepares a case for orphans who have had their land taken from them. Christ is present in the artists from the Chicago suburbs who use the creative gifts that God has given them to represent the pain of brothers and sisters whom they have never seen and to mobilize resources to help them. Christ is present in the sanctuary that gay drug users discover in the presence of a Christian counselor. Christ is present in the millions of Christians who quietly and with little recognition carry the burden of AIDS in their communities and churches around the world. Christ is in the multitude of "ordinary miracles" as women affected by AIDS forgive the husbands who infected them, as youth repent of their self-centered sexual practices, as pastors counsel married couples separated by HIV infection how to use a condom.

In an era of AIDS, Christ is found where he has always been found. He is with the poor, the marginalized, the sinful, the sick and the oppressed. Ransom successfully encountered the Un-man in the blood, sweat, pain and injury of battle. We must encounter AIDS in the blood, sweat, pain and injury of grim reality. Ransom did not defeat the Un-man in the contest of grand ideas and moral argument. We cannot affect the course of AIDS through culture wars. When we are drawn onto our enemy's turf, we are tempted to use his weapons—power against power, spin against spin. When we win, we lose, because we leave behind alienated and wounded people who see only condemnation, competition and judgment in the eyes of Christ's followers.

AIDS ministry is painful, it is long, and it has few tangible rewards. If we are to create a sanctuary for those affected by AIDS, we who minister must also dwell in a sanctuary, in the presence of God:

> Since we have confidence to enter the Most Holy Place by the blood of Jesus, by a new and living way opened for us through the curtain, that is, his body, and since we have a great priest over the house of God, let us draw near to God with a sincere heart in full assurance of faith, having our hearts sprinkled to cleanse us from a guilty conscience and having our bodies washed with pure water. Let us hold unswervingly to the hope we profess, for he who promised is faithful. And let us consider how we may spur one another on toward love and good deeds. Let us not give up meeting together . . . but let us encourage one another—and all the more as you see the Day approaching. (Hebrews 10:19-25)

We recognize that we can enter this Most Holy Place, the dwelling place of God where his glory rests; not because we are good, but because Christ, through his sacrifice, gives us that joy and privilege. If our ministries are to reflect the glory of the God we serve, we must reside in his presence. We do not run into the Holy Place to be equipped for service and then out to serve. We serve from the peace of the Holy Place.

In God's presence, we become aware of our own sin and seek repentance and cleansing. We therefore can serve with the humility of a sinner, and the confidence and strength of a clear conscience. As we encounter our own and others' sexuality, our bodies are released to God's cleansing. We find power to be ever vigilant of our own vulnerability.

Neither the need that we encounter daily nor the love and compassion that we should have for people will be enough to get us through the tough times. We will cycle between compassion and the desire to escape. The compassion that drove us to action will flake away in shards of pain and anger, leaving us raggedly exposed and vulnerable. We will want to don a self-protective cloak of hardness. The hope of Christ, not our own compassion, enables us to persevere. His faithfulness, not ours, is the foundation of ministry.

God must also come to us in one another. Love must take shape in good deeds. For that to happen we must work together, planning and solving problems, and we must meet together, encouraging ourselves in ministry. Our ministry then originates in God, his compassion, faithfulness, love and power. N. T. Wright notes God's participation in our suffering and ministry: "To believe in the Trinity is to believe that God came in Jesus to the place where pain was the greatest, to take it upon himself. It is also to believe that God comes today, in the Spirit, to the place where the pain is still at its height, to share the groaning of his world to bring the world to new life. The Spirit does it by dwelling within Christians and enabling them to stand, in prayer and in suffering, at that place of pain."[7]

When we immerse ourselves in the fight against AIDS at the level of strategy and need, we become frightened by the mismatch between the immensity of the problem and the size of the global response. Our ministries become all but invisible when woven into the tapestry of global need. When we personally encounter AIDS in people and the families affected by it, we are overwhelmed by the suffering that lies behind the frightening statistics. Only as we recognize that the tapestry of response is not emerging by happenstance, but that God is actively weaving us into the fabric of his compassion, are we renewed.

Chrub Goes Home

Chrub was dying. Her grandmother, Sivon, knelt beside her, eyes tearing and hands poised in the Buddhist posture of prayer. Members of the Way of Hope Church who had come to care for Chrub circled her body and clasped her hands. Joke, the director of the AIDS program connected with the church, joined the circle.

"I just want to die. I'm weak and feeling very sick." Chrub said in a breathless, strained voice.

"You'll not die alone, Chrub. We are here with you. Jesus is here."

Chrub nodded. The furrowed brow relaxed.

It was Sunday morning. The volunteers, knowing Chrub's body was giving up, prayed. "Lord, give her your strength and peace. Be with her now."

The volunteers decided to split up, some going to the morning church service with a request to pray for Chrub and Sivon. Others stayed behind to care for Chrub.

It was the church Chrub came to often when she could walk. A big overstuffed chair was in the front row for her to sit, weak with disease but determined to worship her newly found Lord through the music, Scripture and teaching.

The chair was empty this Sunday. By the time the volunteers who had been in Chrub's home got to the church, a runner overtook them, rushed to the front and announced her death.

It wasn't the first death from AIDS the church had experienced, and it wouldn't be the last. Way of Hope Church finds and nurtures many people like Chrub into the hands of God.

The volunteers knew exactly what to do. Time could not be lost. The body had to be cremated before dark because there was no place in the urban sprawl for preserving bodies. Someone contacted the crematorium to make the arrangements. Someone else washed Chrub's body and smoothed her dark curls to frame her silky, whitened face. The men volunteers pounded her coffin together and gently lifted her body onto a mat and into the box. Flowers were found, and the funeral processional was made by motorbike and on foot to the church. All on the very afternoon she died.

At Chrub's funeral, the worship team of the church danced a traditional Khmer dance to the whine and rhythm of Khmer music. The congregation joined in, putting

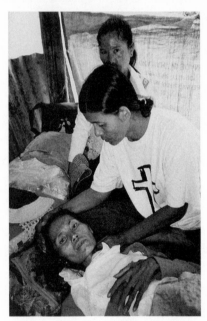

words of praise to traditional song. The church youth performed a drama about AIDS to inform everyone about the disease and how to prevent it. The pastor shared the beautiful gospel of Christ—his death and resurrection—and through him, Chrub's eternal resurrection.

The motorbike and tiny attached wagon pulled up again to the mud-stained cement and corrugated-iron church, and Chrub's body was lowered into the makeshift hearse. The family and church members followed. Many of them had faithfully cared for Chrub for months. They walked in solemn reverence to the designated crematorium on the grounds of a Buddhist temple. As the hearse approached the pyramid-shaped oven, the processional stopped, and the simple wooden box was placed on the wheeled platform.

Sivon was overcome with grief. Supporting her was Joke and other members of the church. They whispered hope into her ears, the same hope Chrub expressed in her life. Chrub's hope transformed her fear of succumbing to AIDS and death into confidence that for her, to live was Christ and to die was certain gain. AIDS lost its sting.

"I believe!" Sivon shouted in her first profession of faith in Christ. "And Chrub, I'll see you again!"

In the face of AIDS, God gives us the direction and wisdom that we need to respond. We have only to equip ourselves for ministry. He desires to sanctify—to set apart as holy—our deepest distress, through his all-sufficient grace. He is our sanctuary and rest. And he will never, no never, no never forsake his children.

Shall AIDS separate us from the love of Christ? No, "for I am convinced that neither death nor life, neither angels nor demons, neither the present nor the future, nor any powers, neither height nor depth, *nor anything else in all creation,* will be able to separate us from the love of God that is in Christ Jesus our Lord" (Romans 8:38-39, emphasis added).

TAKING THE NEXT STEPS

Personal Reflection

1. How did you feel about the discussion of sin in the context of a book on AIDS? What dangers are inherent in discussing the moral and ethical dimensions of personal and structural evil that nurture the spread of HIV infection? What dangers are inherent in avoiding that discussion?

2. Homosexuality represents one of the fronts of our culture wars. All sides of the issue engage the battle with the rhetoric of judgment. Who are the casualties in the culture wars? How have you been wounded? How might you have wounded others? How do you respond to these issues in the privacy of your own thoughts?

3. From whom have you been estranged? How might you reconcile that relationship?

4. To what extent are you open to God's guidance for you personally to become involved with people affected by HIV and AIDS? What barriers or perceived costs prevent that openness?

Action Steps

1. If you have friends who are gay, ask them to tell their stories and listen

openly and without judging. Ask them how they respond to HIV infection and AIDS.

2. If you are living with hatred or bitterness, ask God to help you discern
   where there are broken relationships and how you may be able to pursue reconciliation.

3. Ask God over a period of time how he desires for you to respond to
   the crisis of HIV infection and AIDS, listen for him to respond, and do
   as he directs.

Discussion Questions

CHAPTER 1: UNDERSTANDING THE AIDS PROBLEM

The author recounts being repulsed when meeting an AIDS patient with the purple lesions of Kaposi's sarcoma. It can be very difficult to be around people with the visible signs of any disease, but the fact that AIDS has been portrayed as the result of unclean behavior seems to make it even more difficult.

- How do the physical signs of AIDS make it harder to show compassion to those who are ill?
- To what extent is this a natural response to illness (a desire to protect yourself from infection)?
- To what extent is this reaction informed by the high value our society places on beauty?
- How is this reaction related to our idea of AIDS as a "dirty disease" and a punishment for sexual sin?
- How might a person overcome this reaction?

It is hard for us to imagine the fear and hopelessness that would draw a woman into prostitution, or the desperate poverty that would cause parents to sell their daughter into a brothel. The decisions Chrub's mother made concerning her daughter are hard for us to understand. Yet most of us have sinned out of our own desperation and fear, usually to avoid consequences that were much less serious than starvation. A man may fudge the numbers on a report to avoid missing his goals and losing his job. A woman may spread a juicy rumor about her new neighbor because she is afraid the neighbor may be more popular than she is. And has there ever been a child who never lied to his parents to avoid being punished?

- Have you ever sinned out of fear and desperation?

- How would you feel to have that sin known?
- How did it feel to be desperate?

Chapter 2: AIDS Around the World

It is hard to comprehend the devastation being wrought in Africa and beginning to be seen in Asia. This is partly because we in the Western world have little experience with epidemics, and partly because life in those faraway places seems so different and so foreign it can be hard to relate. Try to imagine what it would mean to have a 10 percent infection rate in America.

- How would it affect your life if you knew 10 percent of your family and friends would become ill and die in the next six to ten years?
- How would it affect your workplace, your neighborhood and your town or city?
- How would it affect the way you thought about AIDS?
- How would you want people in other parts of the world to respond?

Many Asian countries are only now beginning to focus on the AIDS epidemic, even while watching the epidemic boil over in Africa. But it is not just an Asian problem. In the early days of AIDS in the United States, people concerned about the spread of AIDS faced hostility and denial from the government, health-care agencies and the general public.

- Why do you think it is so hard for people to admit that they could possibly get AIDS?
- How might the AIDS epidemic in developing parts of the world affect your life?
- Are there ways that you might be able to respond to the epidemic in other parts of the world?

Chapter 3: Finding Sanctuary

The story of Jesus with the woman caught in adultery shows Jesus providing sanctuary for a woman caught in sin while still telling her to sin no more.

When we follow in his footsteps, we often tread the fine line of loving people without approving of sin. Remembering Christ's response to the woman caught in adultery can help us to hold to that line.

- How would Christ's response have been different if the woman had contracted a disease from her adultery? if the adulterers had been two men?
- Should our reaction to AIDS be influenced by how the person contracted the disease? Why or why not?
- How would it have felt to know that grace was available even though you had done wrong?

In Matthew 22:37-38 Jesus says that the greatest commandment is to love God with all your heart, with all your soul and with all your mind. The second is to love your neighbor as yourself.

- What does this mean in terms of AIDS?
- How far away does someone have to live before they cease to be our neighbor?
- How would you want a family member to be treated if they had AIDS?
- How would you want to be treated if you had AIDS?

CHAPTER 4: PROTECTING OUR YOUTH

Reaching youth is a primary goal of AIDS prevention, and there is some amount of controversy about whether or not youth are capable of remaining abstinent. Young people are frequently represented as being unable to control their behaviors, exercise judgment or make good decisions. Yet in our everyday life we see amazing examples of children and young adults who are focused and goal oriented. Just as every high school has out of control teenagers, they also have teens who are achieving great things academically, in athletics and in the arts—achievements that require a great deal of direction and self-control.

- Do you think it is unreasonable to expect youth to be able to abstain from sex?

- Think of the temptations you faced when you were younger. Were you able to resist them?

- If so, what factors helped you to make a stand? If not, what might have helped you to stand firm?

- What influence did your peer group have in the outcome?

- Do you think the outcome might have been different if you had had different friends?

The book mentions the impact mentors and leaders can have on the behavior of youth.

- How might you go about increasing your impact on the youth in your life?

CHAPTER 5: MINISTRY TO FAMILIES

One of the myths of diseases that are transmitted sexually is that the people with the disease must be guilty of something. Yet statistics tell us that the most common circumstance for a new HIV diagnosis in Africa is a faithful wife being infected by her unfaithful husband.

- How might this change how you think about people infected with HIV?

- What does this say about the importance of strong and stable marriages to social stability?

While many diseases prey on the very young or the old and infirm, AIDS primarily attacks people of reproductive age. This means that the people who are struck down are often the parents of dependent children or the support for elderly parents. While losing any member of a family can be emotionally devastating, AIDS has the additional burden of the cost of extended care and the loss of wage-earners and caretakers.

Think back to when you were a child.

- Were you ever afraid of losing your parents? If so, how did that make you feel?

Think about the first time you lived independently.

- What difficulties did you face?

- How would you have done if you were required to be on your own or the head of a household at 15? 12? What would your life have lacked?
- What do you see as the advantages/disadvantages of keeping orphans in their communities? of placing them in an orphanage?
- How would you feel if you were offered the choice between staying within your community in reduced circumstances, or going away to a more affluent but institutional setting?

CHAPTER 6: AVOIDING THE VIOLENCE OF AIDS

Personal freedom has become a battle cry in our culture. Unfortunately, freedom is often equated with the ability to act without restraint and without facing any consequences. The reality is that our freedom to do what we want to do is curtailed by the reality that behaviors have consequences.

- What are some things you might like to do that you choose not to do because of the consequences?
- Why do you think our culture places so much value on throwing off self-restraint?
- How might exercising restraint where our culture urges excess be an expression of personal freedom?

Behavioral change can be hard. But at some point each of us will face the challenge of having to behave in ways contrary to our inclination. A four year old may spend one day freely playing on the swing set and the next day face the rigors of sitting still in a circle at pre-K. A college senior who rises at noon and throws on shorts and flip-flops may have to get up at 6 and put on a power suit once graduation forces him or her into the work world. And a trip to the doctor has removed cheeseburgers from the diet of many an unwilling soul. Yet successful behavioral change can be an empowering experience that can lead to a lasting feeling of accomplishment.

- What major behavioral change have you faced in your life?
- How successful were you in changing your behavior?

- What factors influenced your success or failure?
- How did your relationship with God help you in your attempts to change?
- When you have successfully changed your behavior, how does it feel?
- What factors make behavioral change a positive experience?
- How is it possible for your example to help others change their behavior?

CHAPTER 7: SHIELDING FROM THE VIOLENCE OF AIDS

Think back to the earlier statement that the most common new HIV infections in Africa occur in married women who have been faithful to their husbands. As Christians we would certainly wish that all people would live in faithfulness to God's laws, and we certainly don't wish to encourage people to believe they can safely sin. However, we must balance this with the knowledge that some people are exposed to risks due to circumstances beyond their control.

- How might it be possible to teach people to remain faithful to God's laws while at the same time teaching them to protect themselves should it become necessary?

One hurdle that Christian AIDS educators face is the idea that it is more immoral to be involved in protected sex than unprotected sex. Some seem to believe that preparedness indicates an intention to sin whereas unprotected sex can be said to "just happen" and thus is a less serious offense.

- What do you think about the idea that sex "just happens"?
- Would you argue that the lack of sexual protection is an indication of good intentions or that it simply increases the potential damage of the act?

Many people feel that they do not need to know how to protect themselves from AIDS because they are not in a high-risk group for the disease. Many people who are now HIV positive once felt the same way.

- Why do you think people are unwilling to think about the transmission of HIV?
- How does this affect the spread of the disease?

- How might you help people become more aware of prevention techniques?

CHAPTER 8: PROVIDING CARE

A current controversy in AIDS has to do with the provision of ARVs to those suffering from AIDS in the Third World. Some believe that it is too expensive to buy and distribute these drugs, while others say that we cannot afford NOT to do everything we can.

- How do you think these decisions should be made?
- How do you think Christ would think about this problem?

Illness is very different in the developing world than it is in more developed countries. The basic health care we take for granted is a luxury in much of the world. Yet the emotions surrounding illness—the fear, the anxiety and the longing for comfort—are universal. The thought of dying helpless and alone is a fearful one for all of us. Think about a time when you were ill, even if it was just the flu.

- Was there someone there to help take care of you?
- If so, what do you remember about their care? Was the impact only physical or was it also emotional?
- How did it make you feel to be cared for?
- If you were alone, how was it to suffer alone?
- How did it influence your feeling of worth?
- What role did your knowledge of God play in how the illness affected you?

CHAPTER 9: AIDS, SEX, SIN AND FORGIVENESS

It is common to see AIDS as the result of sexual sin. Yet in Matthew 5:28 Jesus says that if a man looks at a woman with lust, he has already committed adultery in his heart.

- How does this affect the way we should think about sexual sin?

- If everyone who sinned sexually was equally vulnerable to AIDS, how would the epidemic be different?

An American visiting an African pastor asked if he thought Africa had such serious problems with AIDS because they had a lax attitude toward sexual sin. The African pastor replied, "Every culture has sins it is more accepting of. Fortunately for America, materialism doesn't give you AIDS."

- What kind of sin is in your life that you accept because it is accepted by your culture?

- How do you think God reacts to cultural acceptance of sin?

- How does looking at the sin you tolerate in your own life make it easier to exhibit grace to those involved in sexual sin?

- What would your odds of catching AIDS be if materialism or lying or gluttony caused a disease like AIDS?

Online HIV and AIDS Resources

This selective list includes both Christian and secular sites, some of which may not reflect the values of the authors and publishers.

World Relief has been involved in the fight against AIDS since the mid-1990s and currently works in countries around the world. Their Mobilizing for Life program equips churches and trains local believers to reach out with compassion to their hurting neighbors, demonstrating Christ's love. For more information or to obtain World Relief materials referenced in this book, go to <www.wr.org>. The website also has information about Project 5:16, which teaches and encourages teens to practice abstinence before marriage, and functions as a force for AIDS abstinence education in developing countries.

The HIV/AIDS Bureau of HRSA (The Health Resources and Services Administration) <http://hab.hrsa.gov> provides information on the Ryan White Program, which funds treatment and other services for people living with HIV in the U.S. who have little or no insurance coverage. It also has links to many other sites at <http://hab.hrsa.gov/links.htm>.

The New Mexico AIDS Information Network <www.aidsinfonet.org> provides easily accessible information on HIV/AIDS services and treatments in both English and Spanish, with a huge selection of fact sheets, particularly on treatment.

Links to Aidsinfonet and other fact sheets can also be found via the National Library of Medicine at <www.nlm.nih.gov/medlineplus/aidslivingwithaids.html>.

The International Association of Physicians in AIDS Care has an extensive website with a great variety of AIDS information at <www.thebody.com>.

The Centers for Disease Control and Prevention's AIDS pages (<www.cdc .gov/hiv>) are extensive, with information for professionals and the public, and a link to locate voluntary counseling and testing sites in the U.S. There is an array of fact sheets at <http://www.cdc.gov/hiv/resources/factsheets/index.htm> and prevention information at <http://www.cdc.gov/hiv/dhap .htm>. Their National Prevention Information Network also offers AIDS pages at <www.cdcnpin.org/scripts/hiv/index.asp>.

The International HIV/AIDS Alliance works to reduce the spread of HIV and meet the challenges of AIDS. Publications on effective AIDS programs, including a toolkit for working with orphans and vulnerable children, are available its website <www.aidsalliance.org>.

The Global Fund <www.theglobalfund.org/about/aids/default.asp> was created to finance the fight against AIDS, TB and malaria. Its site lists facts about the global AIDS epidemic.

UNAIDS <www.unaids.org> the Joint United Nations Program on HIV/AIDS, brings together the efforts and resources of ten UN system organizations to the global AIDS response. Their site provides current statistics and trends in the global epidemic and access to publications on best practices.

USAID <www.usaid.gov/our_work/global_health/aids/> administers the U.S. government's overseas AIDS program funding, including implementation of the PEPFAR, the President's Emergency Fund for AIDS Relief.

The World Bank's Center for Global Development website includes HIV/AIDS Monitor pages (<www.cgdev.org/section/initiatives/_active/hivmonitor>) with publications and opinions on the effectiveness of global strategies to fight AIDS.

The Kaiser Family Foundation's websites include <http://globalhealth

facts.org>, which has maps and data on HIV, AIDS, malaria and TB by country <http://statehealthfacts.org>, whose HIV/AIDS pages contain similar U.S. information by state, and <www.kff.org/hivaids/timeline/index.cfm>, which provides history of the pandemic and has links to other information and resources on the main KFF site.

The Federal Drug Administration has an AIDS drug development timeline on its website at <www.fda.gov/oashi/aids/miles81.html>. Related parts of the site contain technical AIDS drug information.

The Johns Hopkins AIDS Service provides technical information for clinicians treating AIDS, but also has an animated illustration of the life cycle of the HIV virus, showing how antiretroviral drugs work <www.hopkins-aids.edu/hiv_lifecycle/hivcycle_txt.html>.

The National Institutes of Health AIDS Information Service <www.aidsinfo.nih.gov> has guidelines; information on antiretroviral drugs, clinical trials and vaccine development; fact sheets and a "tools" section that includes a glossary of HIV/AIDS-related terms.

AEGIS (AIDS Education Global Information System) <www.aegis.org> provides information on a broad range of HIV/AIDS issues, including current news and an online bulletin board.

The American Association of HIV Medicine has a searchable list of HIV specialist physicians at <www.aahivm.org> (click on "Find a provider").

NAM is an organization that offers information across the world to HIV-positive people and to the professionals who treat, support and care for them. NAM's website at <www.aidsmap.org> provides articles, facts and news.

Project Inform <www.projectinform.org> offers AIDS information, including a national information hotline for people with AIDS.

The Global Health Council's website <www.globalhealth.org/aids/> contains an AIDS Action Section with information about spreading the word, influencing Congress, donating to AIDS organizations and volunteering.

DATA (debt AIDS trade Africa) provides action information on contacting leaders <www.data.org/action/tellyourleaders>, telling friends <www.data .org/action/tellyourfriends>, and engaging churches <www.data.org/action/ christianaction>.

The National Association of People with HIV/AIDS <www.napwa.org> is a U.S. organization that advocates to end the pandemic and to alleviate suffering caused by HIV.

The UK Coalition of People Living with HIV and AIDS <www.ukcoalition .org> is committed to enabling the diverse voices of people living with HIV and AIDS to be heard, with a view to influencing change.

The Association of Nutrition Services Agencies <www.aidsnutrition.org> provides support to agencies offering nutrition services to people living with AIDS and has fact sheets on many topics related to nutrition and AIDS, plus nutritional guidelines, on its website.

He Intends Victory, Inc. <www.heintendsvictory.com> seeks to bring spiritual awakening to the HIV/AIDS community and to mobilize and educate the church to respond to people living with AIDS.

The Balm in Gilead <www.balmingilead.org> is an international organization working primarily through African American churches to stop the spread of HIV among the African diaspora.

The National Catholic AIDS Network <www.ncan.org> assists the church in recognizing the pain and challenges of the HIV/AIDS pandemic and in living out its gospel mandate, by offering compassionate support, education, referral and technical assistance.

The Urbana website contains a section with Bible studies called "Ses'khona (we are here): Christ Present in the AIDS Crisis." Written for university students by South Africa's Student Christian Association, the series of eleven studies can be found at <www.urbana.org/_articles.cfm?recordid=688>.

Exodus International <www.exodus-international.org> is a nonprofit, inter-denominational Christian organization that promotes freedom from homo-sexuality through the power of Jesus Christ.

True Freedom Trust <www.truefreedomtrust.co.uk> provides support and resources for Christian men and women struggling with homosexuality.

The International Justice Mission <www.ijm.org> is a Christian human rights agency that rescues victims of violence, sexual exploitation, slavery and oppression around the world.

Saddleback Church desires to respond to the AIDS crisis by interfacing with local and international communities and demonstrating the love of Christ to all in need. You can get more information at <www.saddlebackfamily.com>.

World Vision's Hope Initiative <www.wvi.org/wvi/aids/global_aids.htm> is their global response to alleviate the worldwide impact of HIV/AIDS, through prevention, care and advocacy. Acting on AIDS, a World Vision pro-gram started by Christian college students to create awareness and activism for the global AIDS pandemic at U.S. colleges, is described at <www.world vision.org/aoa.nsf/aids/home?open&lid=aoa&lpos=sitemap>.

Tearfund's International Learning Zone <http://tilz.tearfund.org/Topics/ HIV+and+AIDS> contains "good practice" information for international AIDS programs and a section on AIDS and poverty.

Hope for AIDS <www.hopeforaids.org> is the AIDS initiative of SIM (Serv-ing in Mission). The website has a list of articles and frequently asked ques-tions, as well as information on SIM's AIDS programs.

Viva Network is a global movement of Christians, helping 1.2 million vul-nerable children in 48 countries. Their site <www.viva.org> provides re-sources, contacts and ways to get involved.

The Firelight Foundation <www.firelightfoundation.org> is an organization that supports children orphaned or impacted by AIDS in sub-Saharan Africa through advocacy and strengthening families and communities to care for them.

The Global AIDS Interfaith Alliance <www.thegaia.org> partners with religious organizations in resource-poor countries for community-based HIV prevention and care.

SafAIDS (Southern Africa HIV and AIDS Information Dissemination Service), <www.safaids.org.zw> promotes effective and ethical development responses to the epidemic and its impact, through HIV/AIDS knowledge management, capacity building, advocacy, policy analysis and research.

The Pan African Christian AIDS Network <www.pacanet.net> links churches, Christian organizations and Christian networks to enhance their HIV/AIDS responses by sharing resources, ideas, skills, experiences and stimulating strategic partnerships.

The African Jesuit AIDS Network responds to HIV/AIDS in Africa with appropriate social ministry. As well as describing AJAN's programs, their site <www.jesuitaids.org>, contains commentaries on AIDS in relation to faith, society and communications.

CABASA/CARIS <www.cabsa.co.za> the Christian AIDS Bureau of Southern Africa, hosts the Christian AIDS Resource Information Service, and aims to assist and support churches and faith communities in their involvement in the HIV and AIDS field.

ACET International Alliance <www.acet-international.org> is a global network of organizations working to prevent another generation being devastated by AIDS and to provide help to the sick, dying and bereaved through church mobilization.

Christian HIV/AIDS Alliance <www.chaa.info> is a network of Christian agencies, churches and individuals praying and working together from the U.K. to serve and empower those affected by HIV/AIDS. The site has links to member organizations.

Strategies for Hope Trust <www.stratshope.org> promotes informed, effective, community-based approaches to HIV/AIDS, gender and sexual health, particularly in sub-Saharan Africa, and has a series of practical case studies on AIDS issues.

The Mildmay Mission <www.mildmay.org> specializes in holistic care programs for men, women and children living with HIV/AIDS and other chronic conditions, and develops services and mobilizes others in the fight against HIV and AIDS.

Christian Aid <www.christian-aid.org.uk/hivaids/index.htm> conducts advocacy in the U.K. and funds community-based HIV/AIDS programs internationally.

CANA (Christian AIDS/HIV National Alliance of India) <www.cana-india .org>, mobilizes the Christian community in India to respond to HIV/AIDS. It promotes action through concerned individuals, community-based organizations, churches and NGOs.

Notes

Chapter 1: Understanding the AIDS Problem

[1]Hun Sen, quoted in Ek Madra, "Cambodia Leaders Say AIDS Threat Worse Than War," Reuters NewMedia, March 31, 1999, <http://www.aegis.com/news/re/1999/RE990319.html>.

[2]Stephen Goff, *AIDS and Other Manifestations of AIDS Infection,* 4th ed. (2004), pp. 81-82.

Chapter 2: AIDS Around the World

[1]Susan Hunter, *AIDS in Asia: A Continent in Peril* (Palgrave, N.Y.: Macmillan, 2005), p. 26.

[2]Statistics that we cite in this chapter and throughout the book will change from time to time. To remain current we urge you to consult periodic updates from UNAIDS at <www.unaids.org>.

[3]UNAIDS, 2006 Report on the Global AIDS Epidemic (Geneva: UNAIDS, 2006), p. 15.

[4]UNAIDS, AIDS Epidemic Update: December 2005 (Geneva: UNAIDS, 2005), p. 9 <http://www.unaids.org/epi/2005/doc/report_pdf.asp>.

[5]UNAIDS, 2006 Report on the Global AIDS Epidemic, p. 18.

[6]Unpublished testimony by Nsengiyumva Fidele given at Evangelical Friends Church, Kigali, Rwanda, July 14, 2005.

[7]Hunter, *AIDS in Asia,* p. 27.

[8]ACET International Alliance (London, U.K., 2006) <www.acet-international.org/olga.htm>.

[9]UNAIDS, 2006 Report on the Global AIDS Epidemic, pp. 35-37.

[10]UNAIDS, AIDS Epidemic Update 2005 (Geneva: UNAIDS, 2005), pp. 45-51.

[11]UNAIDS, 2006 Report on the Global AIDS Epidemic, p. 1.

[12]Ibid.

[13]UNAIDS, Caribbean Regional Report, 2005.

[14]UNAIDS, Latin American Regional Report, 2005.

[15]"HIV/AIDS among African Americans," Fact Sheet, Centers for Disease Control (February 2005) <http://www.cdc.gov/HIV/topics/aa/resources/factsheets/pdf/aa.pdf>.

[16]Hannah Manner, story posted at <www.heintendsvictory.com>.

[17]"Black Churches Confront Topic of AIDS," The Body, Centers for Disease Control (March 2002) <http://www.thebody.com/cdc/news_updates_archive/mar8_02/black_church_aids.html>.

[18]Ibid.

[19]Gracia Violeta Ross, address, Ecumenical Pre-conference before the XV International AIDS Conference, Bangkok, Thailand, July 2004.

Chapter 4: Protecting Our Youth

[1]Shelly Clark, Judith Bruce and Annie Dude, "Protecting Young Women from HIV/AIDS: The Case Against Child and Adolescent Marriage," *International Planning Perspectives* 32.2 (June 2006).

[2]Jane D. Brown, Kelly Ladin L'Engle, Carol J. Pardun, Guang Guo, Kristin Kenneavy, and Christine Jackson, "Sexy Media Matter: Exposure to Sexual Content in Music, Movies, Television, and Magazines Predicts Black and White Adolescents' Sexual Behavior," *Pediatrics* 117, no. 4 (2006): 1018-1027.

[3]Ibid.

[4]SIDA is the abbreviation for AIDS in French- and Spanish-speaking countries, from *Syndrome Immunodéficitaire Acquis* or *Síndrome de Inmuno-Deficiencia Adquirida*.

[5]Simon Peter Onaba, "Prevention of HIV/AIDS Among Youth," panel discussion at 15th International Conference on HIV/AIDS, Bangkok, 2004.

[6]*Reach 4 Life* (Colorado Springs: International Bible Society, 2005), p. 24.

Chapter 5: Ministry to Families

[1]BBC Radio News, April 9, 2006.

[2]World Relief, *Our Communities: a Pastoral Counseling Manual for AIDS* (World Relief, 2005).

[3]*National Programme Guidelines on Orphans and Other Children Made Vulnerable by HIV/AIDS* (Nairobi: Kenya Ministry of Home Affairs, March 2002), p. 4.

[4]J. S. Mbiti, *African Religions and Philosophy* (Nairobi: East African Educational Publishers, 1992), p. 109.

[5]Firelight publication

[6]*Children on the Brink 2004: A Joint Report of New Orphan Estimates and a Framework for Action* (UNAIDS, UNICEF and USAID, 2004), p. 20.

[7]Ibid., p. 5.

Chapter 6: Avoiding the Violence of AIDS

[1]Mobilizing Youth for Life is World Relief's program to delay sexual debut and/or reduce the number of sexual partners. The five-year program for Haiti, Kenya, Mozambique and Rwanda is funded by churches, private donors and a USAID grant under the President's Emergency Plan for AIDS Relief (PEPFAR).

[2]Bruce, Judith and Shelley Clark, *The Implications of Early Marriage for HIV/AIDS Policy*, a brief based on a background paper prepared for the WHO/UNFPA/Population Council Technical Consultation on Married Adolescents (June 2004) <http://harrisschool.uchicago.edu/ faculty/ articles/brief6-21-04.pdf>.

[3]2004 Report on the Global HIV/AIDS Epidemic: 4th Global Report (Bangkok: UNAIDS, 2004), pp. 93-100 <http://www.unaids.org/bangkok2004/GAR2004_html/GAR2004_00_en.htm>.

[4]*HIV/AIDS in South Asia* (Washington, D.C.: World Bank, 2005), p. 5.

[5]*Trafficking in Persons Report 2005* (Washington, D.C.: Office of the Undersecretary for Global Affairs, U.S. Department of State, 2005), p. 6.

[6]Interview with Meredith Long, Port-au-Prince, Haiti, 2003.

Chapter 7: Shielding from the Violence of AIDS

[1]Saifuddin Ahmed, Tom Lutalo, Maria Wawer, David Serwadda, Nelson K. Sewankambo, Fred Nalugoda, et al., "HIV Incidence and Sexually Transmitted Disease Prevalence Associated with Condom Use: A Population Study in Rakai, Uganda," *AIDS* 15, no. 16 (November 9, 2001): 2171-2179.

[2]Stephen D. Pinkerton and Paul R. Ambramson, "Effectiveness of Condoms in Preventing HIV Transmission," *Social Science and Medicine* 44, no. 9 (1997): 1303-1312.

[3]Daniel T. Halperin, Markus J. Steiner, Michael M. Cassell, Edward C. Green, Norman Hearst, Douglas Kirby, Helene D. Gayle, and Willard Cates, "The Time Has Come for Common Ground on Preventing Sexual Transmission of HIV," *The Lancet* 364, no. 9449 (November 27, 2004): 1913-1915.

[4]"Male Circumcision," Preventing HIV Infection: Strategic Guidance on HIV/AIDS Prevention: Advances in new Technologies and Issues, United Nations Population Fund (2006) <http://www.unfpa.org/hiv/strategic/advances3.htm >.

[5]*Alcohol Alert # 57: Alcohol and HIV/AIDS* (Bethesda, Md.: National Institutes of Health, September 2002) <http://pubs.niaa.nih.gov/publications/aa57.htm>.

[6]"Universal Precautions for Prevention of Transmission of HIV and Other Bloodborne Infections," Fact Sheet, Centers for Disease Control (revised March 1, 2005) <http://www.cdc.gov/ncidod/dhqp/bp_universal_precautions.html>.

[7]Steffanie A. Strathdee and David Vlahov, "The Effectiveness of Needle Exchange Programs: A Review of the Science and Policy," *AIDScience* 1, no. 16 (December 2001) <http://aidscience.org/articles/aidscience013.asp>.

Chapter 8: Providing Care

[1]*AIDS Epidemic Update: December 2005* (Geneva: UNAIDS, 2005), p. 5 <http://www.unaids.org/epi/2005/doc/report_pdf.asp>.

[2]*UNICEF Procurement of HIV/AIDS-Related Supplies and Services* (Copenhagen: UNICEF Supply Division, April 2005), p. 7 <http://www.unicef.org/supply/files/ARVpaper1.pdf >.

[3]*Hope at Home: Caring for Family with AIDS* (Baltimore: World Relief Corporation, 2000), pp. 22-30.

[4]Though sputum does not carry a threat of HIV infection unless it contains fresh blood, many people with HIV are coinfected with TB or other illnesses that can be spread through sputum.

[5]*Hope at Home*, p. 24.

[6]*Tuberculosis,* Disease Report (Geneva: Global Fund to Fight AIDS, Tuberculosis and Malaria, 2005), p. 24 <http://www.theglobalfund.org/en/files/about/replenishment/disease_report_tb_en.pdf>.

[7]*Malaria,* Disease Report (Geneva: Global Fund to Fight AIDS, Tuberculosis and Malaria, 2005), p. 35 <http://www.theglobalfund.org/en/files/about/replenishment/disease_report_malaria_en.pdf>.

[8]*Hope at Home*, pp. 22-29

[9]W. Meredith Long, *Health, Healing and God's Kingdom: New Pathways to Christian Health Ministry in Africa* (Oxford, U.K.: Regnum, 2000), pp. 201-12.

[10]"A Report of a Theological Workshop Focusing on HIV- and AIDS-related Stigma," (UNAIDS,

2005), p. 31 <www.e-alliance.ch/media/media-5634.pdf>.

[11]N. T. Wright, *For All God's Worth* (Grand Rapids: Eerdmans, 1997), pp. 98-99.

[12]Rite Two, The Holy Communion, *Book of Common Prayer* (New York: The Church Hymnal Corporation, 1979), p. 364.

Chapter 9: AIDS, Sex, Sin and Forgiveness

[1]C. S. Lewis, *Perelandra* (New York: Scribner, 1996).

[2]"Special Focus Profile: Men Who Have Sex with Men," STD Surveillance 2004, Centers for Disease Control, 2005 <http://www.cdc.gov/std/stats/msm.htm>.

[3]W. Meredith Long, *Health, Healing and God's Kingdom* (Oxford, U.K.: Regnum, 2000), pp. 124-30, 229-32.

[4]*Hope at Home: Caring for Family with AIDS* (Baltimore: World Relief, 2000), p. 19.

[5]Lewis, *Perelandra.*

[6]Lynne Hybels, adapted from personal written email communication to Deborah Dortzbach, April 10, 2006.

[7]N. T. Wright, *For All God's Worth,* (Grand Rapids: Eerdmans, 1997), pp. 30-31.